MAMA MOON'S
BOOK OF
MAGIC

IN LOVING MEMORY OF DANDY, FOREVER
IN MY HEART AND THE BEST FAMILIAR
A WITCH COULD HAVE EVER ASKED FOR.

ILLUSTRATIONS BY
NES VUCKOVIC

MAMA MOON'S
BOOK OF
MAGIC

A LIFE-CHANGING GUIDE TO SPELLS, CRYSTALS, MANIFESTATIONS AND LIVING A MAGICAL EXISTENCE

SEMRA HAKSEVER

Hardie Grant

BOOKS

ACTION

+

INTENTION

=

MAGIC

CONTENTS

WELCOME TO MY BOOK

I am always being asked, 'When did you become a witch?' The answer is that I have always been this way. When I consider the path that has led me to where I am, I realise I may not have always identified as a witch but I can't remember a time when I wasn't fascinated and amazed by mystical happenings. Honouring the moon's energy and welcoming amazing signs from the Universe has been my way of life for as long as I can remember.

I've had chance encounters with healers that have influenced my path and I have been lucky enough to have always attracted amazing spiritual friends and teachers into my life.

Over the past 25 years my curiosity about all things metaphysical has inspired me to collect a library and attend many courses on psychic practices, consistently confirming my belief in magic along the way.

So for my third book, it has been both a privilege and a pleasure to write about so many different topics that cover my favourite areas of magic. I'm delighted to have created a cosmic reference book that can assist witches-in-the-making or those interested in dipping a toe into the metaphysical world.

It's incredible to see what happens when people welcome a little magic into their lives. Taking a leap of faith can open up so many amazing and empowering possibilities.

Embracing the spiritual and mystical world brings with it an abundance of gifts, whether it's tuning in to your intuition, connecting to nature's cycles, following the moon's phases, or welcoming signs from the Universe; practising and noticing these wonderful things remind us we are all connected and that magic is *everywhere*!

My favourite type of magic is something that empowers. I believe that when we are feeling good, we transmit positive vibes that create a ripple effect on those around us. From the checkout person at the supermarket to those nearest and dearest to us, I believe that spreading good vibrations can heal the world.

As you turn the pages of this book always remember you are a cosmic force.

Love,

A COSMIC
REFERENCE
BOOK THAT
CAN ASSIST
WITCHES-IN-
THE-MAKING

HOW TO USE THIS BOOK

I have split the book into five parts, to cover all the ways magic can cosmically enrich your life.

PART ONE: THE BASICS

Here, you'll be able to scan through everything you need to get started – a basic magical toolkit, ways to assemble an altar, including one for times when you are short on space or on the go, how to bring your spells and potions to life with hot charcoal discs (a method of burning incense), as well as how to dispel any remnants, and an overview of crystals.

PART TWO: MAGIC IN PRACTICE

Here is where you will find an explanation of the kind of magic that requires candles, spells or potions. Put simply, this is practical magic; a potion for opening your third-eye chakra; a spell to perform when the moon is full to make the most of her heightened powers; or a simple flame-reading exercise to give you a bit of cosmic guidance. You'll also find a guide to the herbs, woods and resins to use in your spells, including a glossary of their magical powers, along with crystal pairings, and information on how to grow, cut and dry your own herbs.

PART THREE: SPIRITUAL SELF-CARE

This chapter is all about your relationship with *you*. One of the most important magical practices you can bring into your life is learning how to manifest, or call things in, and discovering the power of your own intuition. In addition, I've included some lotions and potions including bath and body oils, body scrubs and room vapouriser mixes that act as little spells, whether you need to achieve a moment of inner peace, or invigorate your body and mind for a productive and positive day. Finally, I've set a seven-day magical challenge, which includes ideas for simple ways to incorporate a little magic into the everyday.

PART FOUR: DIVINATION

This chapter is all about fortune telling: what can be divined from practices such as tea leaf and palm reading, tarot using playing cards, DIY oracles and how to interpret signs from the Universe. You first learn to interpret for yourself, and then start sharing with friends.

PART FIVE: CEREMONIES

Ceremonies are a great way of celebrating and strengthening relationships between friends, but are also wonderful ways to explore self-affirmation. I've also included seasonal ceremonies, such as the solstices and equinoxes, to help you harness the powers of nature, whether with loved ones or alone.

WITCHCRAFT 101

I've talked a lot about how to practise magic, but what if your magic isn't working? This section is all about cosmic troubleshooting and problem solving.

HOW TO PRACTISE MAGIC DAILY

The most important thing to remember is that magic should be made to work alongside and around your life. It's about experimenting to see what feels right, and being guided by your own comfort. Saying that, as much as I want you to invite magical moments into your life, it would be wrong to not point out that there is an element of effort required to call things in. Put simply, when the time is right, you will have time for it – and if you don't, you just need to be patient and think about why that is. And remember, this is an opportunity to step away from your phone, your laptop, and any other distractions.

I've found that the simplest way to bring magic in daily is to start small. Recognise that absolutely anything can be a ritual,

from stating an intention when you put your lipstick on, to spending some quality time with your pet or acknowledging nature as you start your commute to work. What more proof do you need that magic exists than noticing the miracles within nature? Even getting up 10 minutes earlier to make a cup of hot water with lemon and look out of the window for a few minutes will set your day on a different path. The most important thing to remember is that this isn't about expectation or pressure – yes, you could burn a self-love spell in the morning, but equally, in the busy hectic lives we lead, we can incorporate the small things in to the same effect – why not establish your daily mantra in the shower? Magic doesn't mean your life will be perfect, but it does give you the best tools to cope with whatever life throws your way. Below you will find a few examples of how I have created ways to incorporate daily practice into everyday life, in the simplest of ways.

RAISING YOUR VIBRATIONS

This will heighten your energy and put you in a positive headspace. Turn to page 116 and get ready to awaken your power.

DAILY RITUAL CHALLENGE

This is an easy way to get in the routine of practising magic daily. I've laid out a full seven-day routine on pages 132–137, which I would encourage you to give a proper go, but, if you're running short of time or energy, then just pick one or two things to try, to give yourself a taste of it.

MOON RITUALS

The number one easiest and most powerful thing you can do is to look at the moon every night. Recognising its phases and how these different stages of its cycle will resonate with how you are feeling is a fast track to understanding the kind of magic that you might want to bring into your routine. For example, when the moon is at its lowest ebb it will likely feel right to hiberate and take a bit of downtime, whether physically, mentally, or both. This might be a time to do a dark moon bathing ritual (see page 82). When the moon is full you might notice that emotionally, things you've been trying to ignore have been cropping up and getting in your way – your intuition may be awakening, in which case turn to page 78 for a full moon bathing ritual. Use these times to really look at yourself, and your needs.

LOTIONS AND POTIONS

Working with a specific incense spell or potion for the week is a great way of turning 10 minutes of effort into something that becomes a benefit all week long. You'll find examples of body oils, vapouriser mixes, body scrubs and bath oils on pages 120–127 that you can make up on a Sunday evening and then use with a daily intention – it can be the same or a different one each day, depending on how you feel.

SIGILS AND SPELLS

Sigils, or personal symbols of intent, and spells, which you will find on pages 114–115, are also great ways to set week-long intentions. You can really experiment with these and make them your own, and again, it requires a little bit of focussed effort and time for a week of magical manifestations. Pick a spell for something specific, then make it last for seven days by speaking your intention as you make your potion, then repeat daily. This is not to be rushed, but the creation of a short-lived habit of the same ritual will help you to strengthen your cosmic power.

MAGIC MOMENTS

Below are a few ways to use magic everyday. Use the lightening bolt rating to guide you through, from instantaneous, feel good magic to magic in less than a minute.

	magic in a minute
	magic in less than 30 minutes
	magic in 1 hour

- Count your blessings – acknowledge three things that make you happy.

- A ripple effect of good vibes – give a stranger a compliment or leave a note of encouragement in a public place and then know that spreading happiness creates a ripple effect.

- Embrace a tree and think about how deep its roots go and admire all the seasons it has lived through.

- Call in on your crystal collection – run your fingers over all of them without looking, find the one that's calling out to you then spend 10 minutes tuning into its energy.

- Call in animal power – go to the park and find an animal, whether that's a dog on a walk, a bird in a tree or a squirrel on the hunt for food, then recognise the magic of its being.

- Look yourself deep in the eyes, in a mirror, and say to yourself 'What can I do for you? What do you need?' Tuning in to yourself is a very deep and transformative experience, which is a great guide to which spells and magic you should be exploring.

- Cleanse your home and welcome in new energy – just as you clean your house physically, you should clean your house energetically, too. See page 44 for smoke cleansing (don't forget to open a window to let negative vibes out).

- Invest in a magical treat – this could be a new-to-you item of clothing or a dish to burn your incense, or a new plant. As you do this, think of what joy you want it to bring into your life.

- Learn a new magical practice – take 1 hour to learn something new, such as cartomancy (see pages 158–168), palm reading (see pages 144–157) or flame reading (see pages 52–53).

THE

BASICS

MAGIC ESSENTIALS

Below you will find a cosmic checklist that will help to get you started. From dressing in a way that makes you feel empowered to knowing which way to stir when you make a potion; these essentials set you on a solid path to your magical destination.

AN OUTFIT OF EMPOWERMENT

I always recommend getting dressed into something that feels empowering when you are about to make a spell and perform a ritual. In doing this you are marking the occasion and acknowledging that you are about to put your intention into something important. Getting a little dressed up can help you focus and be more aware and conscious of the moment. You are performing a ritual that is about to have a massive and positive impact on your life, so your fleece onesie won't cut it! However, if you are performing magic on the move, I suggest that you close your eyes and visualise yourself putting on your imaginary cosmic sparkly cloak. (Don't forget to take it off when the spell is done!)

THE RIGHT HEADSPACE

Before casting a spell, you want to be as calm and as 'in the zone' as possible. Sit comfortably and close your eyes, then take some very gentle breaths in and out through your nose – 5 counts in then 7 or 8 counts out. Repeat this about 10 or 15 times. You can choose to have music on when you are mixing up your magic or do it in silence. Do whatever makes you feel good and focussed and magical.

ENCHANTING AND BLESSING

This means charging a spell with your intention. It is a time to hold your hands over the ingredients of your potion or spell and bless them with your intent. Zone in on your power within, feel light and energy beaming through your fingertips blessing the spell. Visualise the outcome, imagine how you will feel when your magic manifests into reality.

BLENDING

When you blend a spell or potion, remember that you should always stir in a clockwise direction to bring something into your life and in an anti-clockwise direction when you are banishing something from your life.

Always remember, intent is the most powerful ingredient. It is important that you show the Universe that you are willing and that you also have an action plan.

BASIC TOOLKIT

- *Mortar and pestle*
- *Glass jars*
- *Candles in various colours*
- *Crystals (Note: please be sure if you are adding crystals to a tea, tonic, oil or bath that they are polished stones and not raw – the raw ones will tarnish in liquid.)*
- *String of various colours*
- *Parchment or greaseproof paper*
- *Essential oils*
- *Dried herbs*

- *Hot charcoal discs*
- *Tongs*
- *Ceramic/heatproof dish/cauldron/ incense burner*
- *Salt or sand*
- *Compass*
- *And... good intentions*

Most of the herbs that I mention in this book are ones that you may find in your kitchen or are available in supermarkets or online. I always use dried herbs in the spells unless fresh are specified. To cleanse dried herbs before you add them to your spells, crush some sage using a mortar and pestle, and burn it on a hot charcoal disc (see page 20 for full instructions), then pass the herbs through the smoke. (This can also be done with copal resin or frankincense and myrrh.) Once you have done this, you can store them with crystals. If you are unsure which crystals to use, clear quartz is always a good idea.

SUPERPOWER
ACCESSORIES

MOON WATER

Moon water is like holy water to moon worshippers! While the moon is full it is the perfect time to make the most of her shiny beaming rays and soak up her energy. Water that has been charged under a full moon can be used for anything that you think might need a little moon power. You can wash your crystals with it, add it to spells to give them an extra kick, drink it, add it to your bath water, or keep it on your altar (see page 22).

YOU WILL NEED:

- *glass bottle or jug of water (make sure it's filtered water if you plan to drink it)*
- *crystals of your choice (optional)*

Fill a glass bottle or jug with water and leave it outside under the full moonlight to charge it up with the moon's superpowers. Add some crystals to the water for even more power. Bring the water inside before sunrise. Store in a glass jar or bottle.

BLACK SALT

This is a multi-purpose salt that can be used to add superpower to banishing spells, and as a perfect accoutrement for protection spells and for driving away evil.

YOU WILL NEED:

- *salt (sea salt is best, but any salt will do)*
- *charcoal from a hot charcoal disc that has been used in a spell or any burnt sage ash*
- *bowl*
- *spoon*
- *jar to store*

Blend the salt and charcoal in a bowl in an anti-clockwise direction, with a spoon, using your left hand. As you enchant the salt, say out loud, 'I banish you, go away, leave!' Store your black salt in an airtight jar.

MOON SALT

Similar to moon water, this is a way to charge up salt with the full moon's potent rays – it will enhance the salt power in your spells. You can add it to your bath, to cleansing rituals, to protection spells or even use it when cooking.

YOU WILL NEED:

- *bowl*
- *salt (sea salt is best, but any salt will do)*
- *a clear quartz crystal*
- *jar to store*

Leave a bowl of salt and a clear quartz crystal out beneath the moonlight for supercharged protection salt. Bring it in before sunrise and store it in a jar.

HOT CHARCOAL GUIDE

Many of the incense blends (mixtures of aromatic herbs and spices) in this book are to be burned on a hot charcoal disc, and you will need a small pair of tongs for heating these up. If you don't have any tongs, scissors or some tweezers will also do the job. Please don't do this with your hands – the charcoal gets very hot and you don't want to burn yourself (especially before a spell!). For extra insulation, add a generous layer of sand or salt to the heatproof dish you'll be using before you light the charcoal.

Using the tongs, hold the charcoal disc over a flame for 15–20 seconds: when the time is right the charcoal will start sparking. At this point, place the charcoal disc in a heatproof dish filled with salt or sand – this could be an incense burner, heatproof ceramic dish or cast-iron cauldron.

Always place your incense blend a small pinch at a time onto the charcoal disc, being careful not to cover it entirely. You can keep adding the blend as you go on. The charcoal disc will usually burn for around 30 minutes. It will give off a lot of smoke, so make sure you are sitting away from a smoke alarm. You can buy charcoal discs from spiritual stockists, either in shops or online.

HOW TO DISPEL SPELL REMNANTS

If you have made a spell which is inviting or attracting something into your life, bury the remnants (ashes from a paper you've burned, for instance) in your front garden or leave it in a jar by your front door.

If it is for a brand new opportunity or a road-opener, dispose of it at a crossroads that leads in four directions. This can be a little tricky to do, so if you don't have an appropriate junction nearby, you can also dispose of it by burying it near an evergreen tree.

If it is for something that you would like to keep, bury it in your back garden or in a plant pot outside.

If it is something that you would like to banish, bury it somewhere far away from your house, or if it is ashes from paper in a banishing spell, flush it down the toilet, or put it in someone else's bin.

HOW TO BUILD YOUR ALTAR

An altar is your sacred space, a special area where you can sit and meditate, manifest and mix up your potions and spells. You can really decorate as little or as much as you like in this area – it may be somewhere permanently dedicated to being your altar, or it may be a temporary set-up on your kitchen table, where you light a candle. It is entirely up to you. Whatever your set-up, you should arrange the items in your altar (when in use) following the diagram on the page opposite, with the tip of the star pointing out of your house, as this is where the energy flows in and out.

ITEMS THAT YOU COULD PUT ON YOUR ALTAR INCLUDE crystals, candles, any lucky charms you have collected along the way, incense, coins, flowers or some kind of offering (sweets, cake or nuts), angel cards, pictures of anyone special to you or pictures of any gods, goddesses, angels or deities that you feel a special empowering connection with. The one rule I would suggest you follow is to keep your altar away from any electrical items. When you are sitting at your altar, try to have your phone switched off. I know there is always the temptation to post to Instagram and record the event, so if connecting to social media and sharing your ritual with friends is something that is important to you, that's fine. Just try to take a photo at the beginning of your session then switch your phone off so you won't be disturbed and can be fully present in the moment.

SPIRIT/UNSEEN

WATER

AIR

FIRE

EARTH

ALTAR ON-THE-GO

It may be difficult to have somewhere set up permanently, and so a small box provides a neat solution. It's also useful for going to perform a ritual and make magic at a friend's house or outdoors, or if you have pets or children who may access it and knock precious items over, or if you are travelling. You may wish you keep all of your magical props, crystals and tarot cards in there, or perhaps just the essentials. Ideally, it should be surrounded by two candles either side,

an incense burner, a needle and thread with various colour options, and a sprig of rosemary for protection. The essentials should represent all of the elements – earth, air, fire and water – so for example, a vial of water (best if it has been charged beneath a full moon), a vial of earth, a candle, a feather or a wand, an altar cloth, a bell, herbs, tarot cards and crystals. You can choose to use a draw string bag, a wooden box, an old shoe box or a biscuit tin, and you can decorate the box with gem stones or trimmings to make it special.

CLASSICAL ELEMENTS

You may also like to represent the classical elements at your altar. There are four elements, plus the spirit element, which represent the five points of the pentagram.

NORTH = EARTH	For this you can use a bowl of salt, sand or earth from a special place (maybe from beneath one of your favourite trees)
EAST = AIR	Here you can use a feather or smoke from some incense
WEST = WATER	Here you can use some water with some clear quartz crystals in it or, even better, Moon water (see page 19)
SOUTH = FIRE	In this direction, place a lit candle of your choice
THE FIFTH POINT	Represents the spirit or the unseen, which is always above, below and all around us

CRYSTALS

You can also use crystals, to represent the elements. Here are a few of my favourites:

EARTH	Black tourmaline, obsidia, peridot
FIRE	Amber, carnelian, red jasper
WATER	Amethyst, moonstone, celestite, chrysocolla
AIR	Tiger's eye, topaz, lapis lazuli

MAGIC

IN

PRACTICE

HERBS, WOODS AND RESINS

These are gifts from Mother Earth,
filled with an abundance of magical
powers and cosmic healing energy.
They all have specific jobs and
contain a whole lotta vibrations
to assist and guide you when you
are working with them.

INTRODUCTION

Herbs, woods and resins have thousands of years of magical lineage. They are the most crucial element of any potion or spell, and a base knowledge of the 10 most essential magical pairings and their subsequent powers (i.e. a herb, wood or resin with its corresponding crystal) will mean you can have magic at your fingertips at any moment.

These magical ingredients all have different powers, however, all are plant-based. Herbs, of course, are the most familiar and accessible, and it's likely that you will have some growing in your garden or on your windowsill. Woods are simply dried pieces of bark – think cinnamon, sandalwood and cedar. You can get these from spiritual shops or online. As for resins, these are natural gums are extracted from the trunks of trees. Examples of resins include frankincense, myrrh and copal.

In the following pages, you will find information about how to grow, dry and enchant herbs that you have at home. A glossary at the end of the section will explain how to utilise and harness the magical energy of all of these ingredients. You will find them on almost every page of this book, so please refer back to this guide whenever you need to.

'THE QUIETER
YOU BECOME,
THE MORE YOU
CAN HEAR.'

– RAM DASS

10

ESSENTIAL HERBS, WOODS AND RESINS AND THEIR CRYSTAL PAIRINGS

01	**ROSEMARY** (AMETHYST)	Protection, new beginnings, warding off evil, healing trauma, recovery, sobriety
02	**SAGE** (BLACK TOURMALINE)	Clearing negative energy, grounding, banishing bad vibes
03	**LAVENDER** (CARNELIAN)	Healing, calming, relaxing, personal blessings
04	**CINNAMON** (RED JASPER)	Action, clarity, guidance, focus
05	**ROSE PETALS** (ROSE QUARTZ)	Universal love, self love, receiving love, giving out love – everything love!
06	**THYME** (CLEAR QUARTZ)	Paving the way, cleansing negative energy, intuition, fresh starts
07	**BASIL** (CITRINE)	Prosperity, abundance, manifesting and calling in security, safety, new opportunities, courage
08	**BAY LEAVES** (AZURITE)	Personal power, achieving goals, staying focussed
09	**FRANKINCENSE** (LABRADORITE)	Connecting to the spiritual world, psychic visions, connecting to your guides, the unseen
10	**ALLSPICE** (EMERALD)	Luck, abundance, inspiration, good fortune

PLANTING, CUTTING AND DRYING HERBS

PLANTING HERBS

Growing your own herbs is not only good for the soul and emotionally satisfying, it also intensifies the plants' magical properties, manifesting good things from the get-go. What's more, biodynamic gardening – or following the lunar calendar on when to sow and harvest your plants – is fully organic and believed to result in bigger, healthier crops.

You'll need to look up specifics for the herbs you decide to grow, but the premise for creating spell-binding plants is the same:

01 The best time to plant is during the new or waxing moon phase (see pages 74–75).

02 Hold the seeds or cuttings in your hands and visualise them growing into big, beautiful, healthy plants.

03 Add compost to a pot to suit the size of your cutting or seed – it's better to use terracotta than plastic because it holds moisture in the soil more effectively. If your pot doesn't have holes in the bottom, put a handful of small rocks or pebbles in first to help the soil to drain.

04 Once potted, touch the soil with your fingers, close your eyes and imagine your energy being absorbed into the soil, while focussing on what you want to manifest, be it a financial happening or a romantic tryst – your plants will grow alongside your dreams.

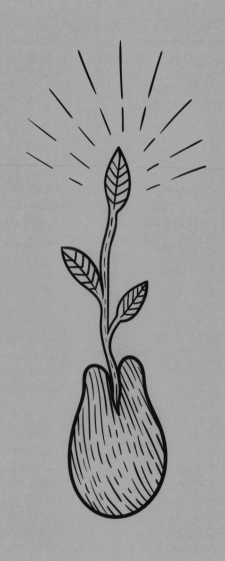

05 Choose a crystal to keep your plant company and place it gently on top of the soil.

06 Water in a clockwise direction and continue to do so for the life cycle of the plant.

07 Finally, give your plant a name.

CARING FOR YOUR HERBS

Think of your herb plants as your little green friends – they love company just as much as people do.

Talk to them daily, ask how they are – you'll begin to recognise when they are thirsty, when they need a little more sunlight or to have a rest in the shade. And if you don't feel like talking, why not make them a playlist, as I do. Mine love Kate Bush and Florence and the Machine, even old-school hip hop.

HOW TO CUT YOUR HERBS
When harvesting, it's important to honour the plant: give thanks for it growing and always ask its permission before you make a cutting.

01 The best time to cut plants is when the moon is waning (see page 81); so if you can, wait for this moment (but obviously, if you have a magical emergency and need a cutting, you can do so at any time – just remember to thank your plant accordingly). If cutting from an outdoor plant, make sure the morning dew has evaporated from the leaves.

02 Prepare a magic knife or scissors by thanking them for their help and anointing them with frankincense.

03 Now to cut. As above, confirm permission, and thank the plant afterwards.

HOW TO DRY HERBS

ALL YOU WILL NEED IS:

- *cotton string or natural twine*

01 Gather your herbs and pat them dry with a cloth to remove any dew.

02 Lay them down on a flat surface. Using your twine, wrap and tie the bundle at the base with a secure knot.

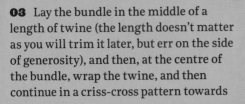

03 Lay the bundle in the middle of a length of twine (the length doesn't matter as you will trim it later, but err on the side of generosity), and then, at the centre of the bundle, wrap the twine, and then continue in a criss-cross pattern towards the top. Do this tightly, but not so tightly that you crush the herbs. As you cross the twine, use the opportunity to programme the herb bundle with your intentions for its eventual purpose.

04 Tie in a knot at the top, then hang the bundle upside down in a cool and dry place for a week, or until the herbs are fully dry.

05 Use these herbs to either burn as a bundle (see pages 44–45), or untie and store in a mason jar for use in incense spells, which you'll find throughout.

ENCHANTING HERBS

Whether you are using them fresh, dried or in the form of an oil or resin, preparing your magical ingredients and programming them (which you will learn about in the following pages) is important so that they know what job they are being asked to do.

Enchanting them is vital and it can be done on many levels... The bigger the blessing the more energy you will harness from them.

If you are a witch on the go, need to perform a spell in a hurry and don't have time to do the full blessing, you can whisper your intention to the herbs or hold your hands over them and tell them what you are using them for. For full enchanting action, it's a good idea to bless in bulk. Choose your essential herbs (see page 33) and store them in glass jars with crystals for company.

Firstly, you may like to cleanse your herbs of any negative energy they may have picked up, as you never know what their journey to the supermarket shelves has been like and what kind of energy they may have encountered.

HOW TO CLEANSE YOUR HERBS

Cleanse herbs by burning sage under them (you can do this over some sage burning on a charcoal disc, see page 20.

As they are bathed in the smoke say something like:

'Allow this smoke to clear any negative energy that these herbs may have encountered on their way to me.' Or 'These herbs are now pure and free spirits – please assist in cleansing these herbs of any stagnant and negative energy.'

Always remember:
If you are saging, it's always a good idea to burn something else afterwards. This is because as the sage clears away negative energy it leaves a space, I always like to fill that space with an intention or blessing so that there is no room for negativity to return.

HOW TO BLESS YOUR HERBS

Magical Herbal Blessing Smoke:
Blend 3 pinches of cinnamon, 1 pinch of rosemary and ½ teaspoon of dragon's blood resin. Blend and burn them on a charcoal disc (see page 20). Bathe the herbs through the smoke and tell the herbs that you bless them with love and good intentions.

Full Moon Blessing:
Lay your herbs out beneath a full moon surrounded by your favourite crystals and candles. Ask the moon to shine brightly and send cosmic magical moon power to your herbs.

Summer Solstice Blessing:
This is the ultimate time to bless your herbs. It is the day when the sun is out for the longest and is sending down the most powerful cosmic rays of light.

For this ritual, set up an altar facing east - the direction of the rising sun. Lay out all of your herbs, charms and crystals a little before sunrise. Ring a bell or play a sound bowl over them to wake them up, so they can soak up the magical solstice sunshine. Look up and thank the sun for shining down and helping all of these magical herbs grow under its golden rays.

HOW TO STORE YOUR HERBS

Store your herbs in glass jars, add extra magical items such as charms, crystals, notes of intent and sigils to power them up.

HERB, WOOD AND RESIN GLOSSARY

ALLSPICE
Good fortune, money, healing, uplifting. Gives extra power and good energy to any spells.

BASIL
Peace, happiness, money, personal wealth, luck, protection, blessing.

BAY LEAVES
Protection, good fortune, psychic awareness. Brings positive change, magical power to spells. A powerful messenger when spells and sigils are written on them.

BENZOIN
Purification, eases stressful situations, banishes anger, adds speed and a bit of oomph to spells. Good for when picking a tarot or angel card. Boosts energy and focus.

BERGAMOT
Brings happiness, luck, assertiveness, courage and motivation.

CARDAMOM
Brings courage and luck, road-opener, grounding.

CAYENNE PEPPER
Removes obstacles and blockages, road-opener, brings opportunity and speeds things up.

CEDAR
Personal success, wealth, healing, wisdom and balance.

CHAMOMILE
Money, success, luck, new beginnings, love.

CINNAMON
A positive blessing for yourself and your home. Love, passion, prosperity, personal strength and psychic awareness.

CLOVES
Luck, courage, self-belief, personal growth, lust.

CUMIN
Healing, protection, love, lust, breaking hexes, new beginnings and emotional strength.

DAMIANA
Aphrodisiac and heart-opener when brewed. Opens the psychic portals when burnt.

DRAGON'S BLOOD
Super-powers good fortune, grants wishes, increases potency and draws luck to any spell.

EUCALYPTUS
Purification, cleansing, clears negative psychic energy. Healing and protection.

FENNEL
Courage, protection, aphrodisiac. Reverses hexes and negative spells.

FRANKINCENSE
An offering to spirits, spiritual cleansing, consecrating magical tools.

GALANGAL
Assists you to take action and provides psychic energy to help you to get up and go (so be careful if you burn it at night). Mental power, assists with communication and willpower. Can support with psychic visions.

GINGER
Romance, prosperity, passion, power. Can be used to speed up spells.

JUNIPER BERRIES
Magical power, protection, control, ending negative and stressful situations.

LAVENDER
Happiness, strength for relationships, psychic awareness, inner strength, psychic power, peace, meditation.

LEMON
New beginnings, cuts hexes, cleansing.

LEMONGRASS
Road-opener, breaks down creative blocks and inspires creativity, brings good luck in communication.

MARJORAM
Protection, psychic awakenings, attracts love.

MUGWORT
Drink for astral projection, protection, third-eye awakening, to help you focus while making spells.

MYRHH
Psychic vibrations, offering to spirits, protection, blessing, healing. Increases power of any healing spell.

NUTMEG
Prosperity, good fortune, love, psychic power.

ORRIS ROOT
Assists with personal power and success. Communication with loved ones and colleagues. Can be used to invite a lover into your life.

PATCHOULI
Works as a magnet for good things. Prosperity, love, fertility.

PEPPERMINT
New beginnings, personal renewal, psychic protection, release, healing, decision-making.

ROSE PETALS
Love, romance, friendship, lust, peace, happiness, relaxation, self care.

ROSEMARY
Protection, purification, healing, mental power, connecting to your intuition and third eye, good health, healing.

SAGE
Healing, purification, cleansing, banishing negative energy, spiritual health.

SANDALWOOD
Healing, awakening psychic ability, luck, success, an offering to the spirits, powerful in moon-related spells. The smoke of sandalwood carries your intentions and manifestations out to the Universe.

STAR ANISE
Psychic awareness, third-eye opener, astral projection, luck, keeps away evil.

THYME
Strength, courage, wisdom. Helps you to connect and trust your inner voice. Attracts loyalty and friendship.

VETIVER
Peace of mind, overcoming fear, breaking hexes, banishes negativity.

YARROW
Psychic awareness, banishes negativity, faithfulness in love, peace and diffusing anxiety.

SMOKE CLEANSING

Burning herbs, woods and resins has been used for thousands of years, from early witchcraft and paganism to ancient Egypt, and from the Catholic Church to Native American ceremonies.

Whether they were burning herbs, resins or wood, smoke has been used in spiritual practices to purify, cleanse and energetically hit the reset button.

Smoke works as a spiritual detergent, reaching all those stagnant energetic stains that we can't see!

As the smoke travels through the air and floats through the atmosphere it is charged with your magical intention, whether that might be clearing toxic vibes and negative energy, blessing yourself and your space, or as an offering to your spirit guides.

To invoke its full power, it is always important to focus and to dedicate your complete intention into the smoke. Talk to it as it travels and guide it to bring healing and transform the energy around you and your space.

You may choose to blend your herbs and create an incense that can be burnt on hot charcoal (see page 20), or create herb bundles from home dried plants (see pages 38–39) or fresh home grown herbs.

A couple of important things to remember:

- A smoke cleanse can sometimes be confused with the term 'smudging'. Please be aware that smudging is a sacred ceremony which is specific to Native American cultures. Always remember to honour and be conscious of a ritual's origin.

- Palo santo is endangered, and white sage, though not endangered, comes from a habitat that is under threat, so if you are buying a premade bundle please check its contents for endangered species, as it's not cool and totally unmagical to purchase plants that are close to extinction.

HERBS TO BURN AND THEIR MEANINGS

CEDAR: Success, wealth, balance.

CINNAMON: Blessing, passion, personal strength.

LAVENDER: Happiness and healing, purification, psychic protection.

MINT: Prosperity and luck, cleansing.

MUGWORT: Astral projection, psychic dreams, removes negative energy, stimulates dreams, divination.

OLIVE LEAVES: Grounding, cleansing negative energy.

ROSEMARY: Protection, new beginnings, healing, third eye awakening.

ROSE PETALS: Love and peace, happiness.

SAGE: Cleansing negative energy, protection, purification.

HOW TO MAKE A HERB BUNDLE

You'll find instructions for drying herbs on pages 38–39, but you can also gather a selection to create bundles with specific intentions.

- *Negative energy*
Rosemary, olive leaves

- *Bless yourself and your surroundings*
Rose petals, lavender, cinnamon

- *Bring prosperity*
Rosemary, cinnamon, mint

- *Bring peace*
Rose petals, cinnamon, thyme

- *Bring love*
Rosemary, rose petals, cinnamon

CANDLE
MAGIC

The magical power of a candle
is its ability to represent all of
the elements: the flame, fire; the
melted wax pool, water; the solid
wax, earth; and the smoke, air.

INTRODUCTION

A candle is, effectively, lighting a fire in your house; it requires your complete attention and focus. The flame demands you to honour it, take time and be in the moment with it.

You can use a candle to light the path that will guide you towards your future and assist you with your magical workings, or burn away what is no longer serving you.

I strongly feel that a candle is the most accessible way of bringing magic into your life, which is why I began my business, Mama Moon Candles. By honouring the flame and calling in scent magic, you can connect to what you want to call in and manifest, allowing the power of the scent to present an offering to the spirits and energy around you to attract, inspire and bring good fortune.

On the following pages, you will discover how to utilise candles to do everything from casting spells to reading the messages that the flame is communicating to you.

HONOUR
THE
FLAME

USING CANDLE MAGIC

Candles are magical, mystical multifunctional tools.

A hypnotising flame that keeps you still in the present moment, turning darkness to light, always changing its shape, reminds us of transition and transformation.

Each of nature's elements is represented:

EARTH
is represented
by the
candle wax

WATER
is represented
by the melted
wax pool

FIRE
is represented
by the flame

AIR
is represented
by the smoke

When creating a candle spell you can begin with the colour of your candle. Colours carry different vibrational frequencies, so choose the colour of your candle to bring extra energy to your spell. If in doubt, a white candle is multifunctional.

CANDLE COLOURS:

BLACK	Banishing, breaking hexes, grounding
BLUE	Calming, healing, meditation, peace, forgiveness, inspiration
GREEN	Success, money, prosperity, freedom, abundance, good luck
ORANGE	Ambition, courage, luck, new beginnings
PINK	Romance, affection, friendship, devotion, emotional healing
RED	Love, passion, power, attraction, fast action, willpower, courage
WHITE	Cleansing, truth, protection, new beginnings
YELLOW	Creativity, learning, communication, road opener, concentration

EASY PEASY

Candle spells can be as easy as lighting a flame while you focus on your intention. Allow it to take a prominent place in your mind and visualise it while staring at the candle flame. As you stare at the flame soften your gaze, allow yourself to be hypnotised by the flame, focus on sending the energy of your intention to the flame.

Notice how the flame is moving – it might be trying to send you a message (see page 52).

DRESSING A CANDLE

When you dress a candle, you are anointing it with the help of magical herbs and oils that are going to work to attract what you are calling in.

To dress a candle, first anoint it with some oil. Olive oil is great if you are also adding herbs, as they stick well to it, but any oil is fine. You can choose to blend a few drops of essential oil with this oil as part of your spell too. Rub the candle with the oil in an upwards direction if you are calling something in and a downwards direction if you want to banish something.

Blend the herbs that correspond to your spell (in a clockwise direction) and then lay them out. Roll the candle in the herbs so the candle is dressed with the herbs.

Refer to the glossary on pages 42–43 to create your own magical blends to anoint your candle with.

You may also choose to carve a sigil (see pages 114–115) or a word, which states your intention, into your candle, or you can write out your intentions on a piece of paper and place it under the candle with the words facing upwards.

It is important to visualise what you want to call in as you dress the candle – feel the emotions of how you will feel when the spell works (for a little bit of guidance, turn to pages 106–117 for more on how to manifest). Visualise your end goal. Remember that when you do this you will be emitting magical magnetic energy that will attach itself to the spell.

Additionally, you can choose to decorate the area around the base of the candle – creating a magic circle around it using rose petals, rice, salt, rosemary and crystals. Again, choose whatever feels right and corresponds with the spell.

BURNING A CANDLE

How long you burn the candle for is up to you. You may wish to burn the candle for a few hours each evening over several nights or you may wish to burn it all in one go.

When the whole candle is burnt, the spell is ready. To dispose of the spell remnants, see page 21.

PYROMANCY *aka* FLAME READING

You can interpret the outcome of your spell by paying attention to the way a candle flickers and melts. This can be a significant and powerful message. Pay attention to the flame as it might be trying to communicate with you.

IF YOUR CANDLE...

Burns bright, clean and with an even melt:
This is a good sign, it represents everything is happening according to plan and that your spell will work. It will happen easily, but might not happen as fast as you would like.

Burns with a big strong flame or if the flame is flickering towards you:
The energy in your spell is super-strong, roads are opening for you, everything will come easily with very little resistance. Expect good news fast!

Burns with a flickering flame:
A flame that flickers fast could mean that your spirit guides are around you, they are watching out for you and the flickering flame is them letting you know that your manifestations have been heard. Say 'Hi' to them, ask them if they can send you some signs (in my experience they are more than happy to do this, so keep your eyes open for the messages they will bring you).

Burns with a flame that resists going out or reignites:

This spell isn't ready to be put out – try focusing on your intention a little longer. This could also mean that some magic was being worked at that exact moment and it needs to burn some more.

Burns with a small flame or a flame that flickers away from you:

Your spell is going to work, but will probably go a little slow. You might face a few obstacles along the way. This isn't necessarily a bad thing. Remember, timing is everything!

You can experiment when the flame is like this: try closing your eyes and visualising a little harder. Try to send more energy to the spell. As you do this, imagine being bathed in warm, golden light and magical energy radiating around you. It's very likely that when you try this, the flame will get bigger.

Burns with a tiny flame:

If the flame is struggling to stay lit, take it as a sign that this spell may not be the right one for you. Have a little rethink – are you really asking the best for yourself right now? Tune into yourself. If you have the slightest feeling in your tummy that you shouldn't be asking for this, stop immediately.

Burns with a crackling or popping sound:

The spirits are trying to send you a sign and communicate with you.

Burns out before the spell is finished:

Take this as a sign that you shouldn't be doing this spell. Whoever is watching over you is taking control and you should take notice, this is not to be ignored.

Burns with an asymmetrical melt:

This is a sign that you need to balance some aspects of your life before your spell can work.

Disclaimer: Please check all of these things before you start to download messages from you flame:

- A tall flame can be caused by an untrimmed wick.
- Black soot is the result of oils or colourants being exposed to high heat, so probably isn't a sign.
- Keep the candle away from a direct draft.

EXTINGUISHING THE FLAME

Many people say that during spell work with candles you shouldn't blow them out and you should, instead, clap over it with both your hands. I have always thought that blowing out candles is much like blowing out candles on a birthday cake and making a wish. When you do this you can also watch the smoke travelling and know that it is carrying your intention out to the Universe. So just do whatever feels right!

CHAKRA MAGIC

Chakras are cosmic portals that
run through the centre of your
body, from the top of your head
to the base of your spine. They are
the connective energy channels
between our physical and spiritual
self, working as psychic filters
to balance our energy fields.

INTRODUCTION

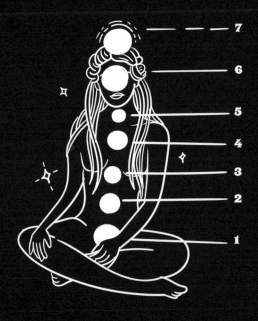

Chakra is the word for 'wheel' in the Sanskrit language. To imagine how they work, imagine a cosmic wheel of energy spinning, creating a vortex of energy which connects your body to the Universe.

There are seven main chakras:

1   *Root Chakra*
2   *Sacral Chakra*
3   *Solar Plexus Chakra*
4   *Heart Chakra*
5   *Throat Chakra*
6   *The Third-eye Chakra*
7   *The Crown Chakra*

Each is connected to emotional, physical and spiritual areas your life. They absorb and filter all of your thoughts, actions and behaviours, and soak up from and react to people and energy around you.

When we come into contact with negative energy and the stresses and struggles of everyday life, there is a good chance that your chakra energy fields may have been whirling and swirling on overtime. When this happens, these magical energy portals can get a little bit clogged up and worn out. You may find that this can slow you and your magic down. You may notice that you are feeling a bit foggy, are unable to make decisions, are having problems connecting to others or are finding it hard to be able to speak up for yourself. You may engage in negative-self talk, or feel a sense of shame, to name a few.

These could be signs that your chakras may need a little bit of TLC.

Over the next few pages are the crystals and potions you need to help get those wheels whirling around and aligned and flowing with all the good energy.

ROOT CHAKRA

The root chakra, as you might imagine, is connected to grounding; this can help you re-establish, or strengthen, your connection to Mother Earth.

01 Mix the carrier oil with the essential oils in a small glass bottle with a dropper lid.

02 Take the oil, rub it on the base of your spine (it is best to be sitting up for this one), and as you do so, hold the crystal and repeat the mantra.

03 Visualise your roots coming out of your spine and flowing into the ground beneath you, feeling the energy gently tying you to the Earth's centre.

LOCATION:	The base of your spine
JOB:	Keeping you stable, grounded and secure
BLOCKS:	Guilt, fearfulness of life
COLOUR:	Red
CRYSTALS:	Black tourmaline, obsidian, red jasper, smoky quartz
POTION:	50 ml (2 fl oz) of a carrier oil of your choice, 10 drops of sandalwood and 5 drops of patchouli essential oil
MANTRA:	I am here, I am safe, I am grounded

SACRAL
CHAKRA

The sacral chakra is often associated with sensuality, whether that is an awareness of your own intents and desires, or a recognition of yourself as a powerful being. This ritual will engage yourself... with yourself.

01 Mix the carrier oil with the essential oils in a small glass bottle with a dropper lid.

02 Take the oil, rub it just below your pelvis, and as you do so, hold the crystal and repeat the mantra.

03 Visualise an orange light pouring into this area and filling up your body with good feelings, knowing that you are worthy of all good things.

LOCATION:	Your pelvis (below the navel)
JOB:	Related to your sexuality, dreams and desires... also connected to your hormones
BLOCKS:	Physical trauma, low energy
COLOUR:	Orange
CRYSTALS:	Carnelian, moonstone
POTION:	50 ml (2 fl oz) of a carrier oil of your choice, 10 drops of lemon and 5 drops of patchouli essential oil
MANTRA:	I am comfortable in my body

SOLAR PLEXUS CHAKRA

This chakra is all about personal empowerment and positive energies. Use this ritual in moments where you need to call on your inner strength.

01 Mix the carrier oil with the essential oils in a small glass bottle with a dropper lid.

02 Take the oil, rub it on your solar plexus, and as you do so, hold the crystal and repeat the mantra.

03 Visualise yellow light entering your chakra and surrounding your body, flooding it with its powerful energy.

LOCATION:	Above your navel
JOB:	Self-esteem and confidence, power and self-worth. Good to connect to when manifesting your destiny
BLOCKS:	Fear of being out of control, low self-esteem, lack of trust
COLOUR:	Yellow
CRYSTALS:	Citrine, tiger's eye
POTION:	50 ml (2 fl oz) of a carrier oil of your choice, 10 drops of lavender and 5 drops of lemon essential oil
MANTRA:	I am worthy of good things

HEART
CHAKRA

The heart chakra is, unsurprisingly, all about love. This is a great ritual if you feel like there might be a blockage holding you back from opening yourself up emotionally.

01 Mix the carrier oil with the essential oils in a small glass bottle with a dropper lid.

02 Take the oil, rub it on your heart and as you do so, hold the crystal and repeat the mantra. You can also follow the friendship circle group tea ceremony on pages 200–201 alongside this.

03 Visualise a green, powerful light surrounding you with loving energy and support.

LOCATION:	Your heart!
JOB:	Helps with love, compassion and healthy relationships. The ability to give and receive love. Joy and inner peace
BLOCKS:	Heartache, grief, lack of compassion
COLOUR:	Green
CRYSTALS:	Rose quartz, emerald green calcite
POTION:	50 ml (2 fl oz) of a carrier oil of your choice, 10 drops of rose and 5 drops of lavender essential oil
MANTRA:	I am open to give and receive love

THROAT CHAKRA

Clearing your throat chakra will help you to communicate and break your internal boundaries.

01 Mix the carrier oil with the essential oils in a small glass bottle with a dropper lid.

02 Take the oil, rub it at the centre of your collarbone and as you do so, hold the crystal and repeat the mantra.

03 Visualise a blue light travelling through your throat, thinking about what you want to say.

LOCATION:	The centre of your collarbone
JOB:	Expressing yourself, self-respect, connecting to your inner voice
BLOCKS:	Creative blocks, losing your voice and repressing emotions
COLOUR:	Blue
CRYSTALS:	Lapis lazuli
POTION:	50 ml (2 fl oz) of a carrier oil, 10 drops of rosemary essential oil and a pinch of thyme
MANTRA:	I communicate with ease and am always understood

THE THIRD-EYE CHAKRA

This chakra helps you to engage with your inner wisdom; knowledge is power both within and without.

01 Mix the carrier oil with the essential oils in a small glass bottle with a dropper lid.

02 Take the oil, rub it between your eyebrows and as you do so, hold the crystal and repeat the mantra. Tune into yourself and see what messages come up.

03 Visualise an indigo light beaming out of your third eye and guiding you to the questions you seek answers to.

LOCATION:	Between your eyebrows
JOB:	To tune into your intuition and connect to your spiritual side
BLOCKS:	Closed mindedness, lack of using your intuition
COLOUR:	Indigo
CRYSTALS:	Amethyst, obsidian, lapis lazuli
POTION:	50 ml (2 fl oz) of a carrier oil of your choice, 10 drops of lavender essential oil and 5 drops of sandalwood essential oil
MANTRA:	I hear and trust my inner voice

THE CROWN CHAKRA

Follow this ritual to unblock the crown chakra if you are feeling a little out of sorts, but are not sure why.

01 Mix the carrier oil with the essential oils in a small glass bottle with a dropper lid.

02 Take the scented shampoo and rub into your scalp, massaging your crown, repeating the mantra at the same time.

03 As you apply the shampoo, visualise a purple light coming in through your head and spreading out in your fingertips, surrounding your body and welcoming in the cosmic energy.

LOCATION:	At the top of your head
JOB:	To connect us to the Universe and trust in ourselves
BLOCKS:	Anger, disconnection from other people
COLOUR:	Purple
CRYSTALS:	Clear quartz, moonstone, labradorite
POTION:	Add 2 drops of peppermint oil and 2 drops of rose oil to the usual amount of unperfumed shampoo that you use to wash your hair
MANTRA:	I am a portal for cosmic energy

MOONOLOGY

The moon. Our magical, mystical
silver orb of wonder in the sky!

INTRODUCTION

A miraculous mighty force of nature, the moon was formed around 4.51 billion years ago as a result of a major collision between earth and the planet Theia. The crash was so powerful it shifted the position of Earth's axis to be at the most perfect point to synchronise and work with the moon to help create seasons, and provide a gravitational pull so strong it controls the tides.

How mind-blowing to look up and bathe in Mama Moon's cosmic beams of light and take a moment to realise that this colossal encounter created this crucial satellite that ensures the stability of the earth's spin and which formed in the perfect place to be illuminated by the sun and provide us with light at night.

The magical power of the moon's energies is undeniable and was recognised around the world in ancient sacred ceremonies. Its cycle has been used as a guide to the harvesting of plants and trees.

Often we can feel the moon's cycle having an effect on our own energy and emotions. This is because the moon influences us in the same way it does the sea. Just as it has the power to move huge bodies of water, the human body is made up of mostly water (about 60 per cent) and just as Mama Moon's strong gravitational pull controls the tides of the ocean, she creates waves within us, affecting our sleep patterns, energy levels, menstrual cycles and moods.

MOON CYCLES

I have found that when you start to acknowledge the deep connection that we have with the moon, it works as a super-powerful reminder that we are all cosmic beings connected to nature. This gives us all the more reason to work with the moon phases on both an emotional and magical level.

WHEN WE WORK ALONGSIDE THESE LUNAR CYCLES WE CAN ELEVATE OUR MAGIC TO THE HIGHEST POWER.

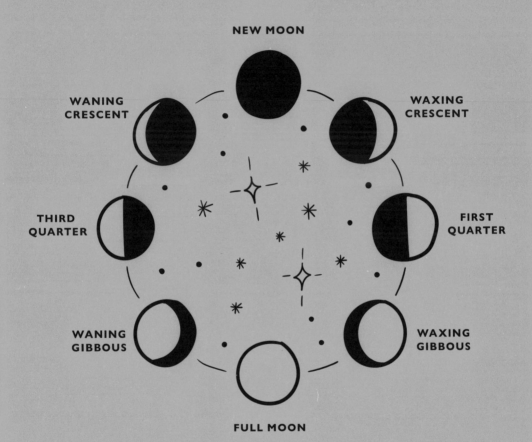

NEW MOON

New moon energy is the perfect time to work with new beginnings. This is a time to think about what it is that you want to call into your life. How do you want things to be? Emotionally, physically, romantically, spiritually?

If you have been procrastinating about starting a new project, hobby or business idea, use this moon energy to give you the courage to start whatever it is. Make a date with yourself in your diary and set aside the time to focus on this new beginning.

Maybe you have an intention to exercise? Or start dating? This is the time to do it.

PERSONAL POWER POTION

YOU WILL NEED:

- *5 cloves*
- *1 pinch of thyme*
- *1 bay leaf (with a sigil on it for super-power, see pages 114–115)*
- *5 drops patchouli essential oil*
- *a mortar and pestle*

01 First, blend all the dry ingredients using a mortar and pestle to a fine powder.

02 Next, add the patchouli oil and blend in a clockwise direction into a paste.

03 Follow the hot charcoal guide on page 20 to create your spell.

WAXING CRESENT

The waxing cresent is somewhere between the new moon and its first quarter; take this as a sign of what to expect magically in this phase.

This is the moment that you refocus on calling things in. All those things you manifested at the turn of the new moon should shift to establishing what you want, to visualising your perfect lifestyle.

How do you see your ideal day? What's your job? What are you doing socially? Whatever your heart desires, no matter how big or small, tune into it, notice how this feels in your body, take time to dream, imagine it as a colour. Feel this colour wash over you, write it all down and set your intentions.

SYNCHRONICITY SPELL

YOU WILL NEED:
• *1 pinch of frankincense* • *1 star anise* • *2 pinches of dried rosemary* • *a mortar and pestle*

01 Blend the ingredients to a fine powder in a clockwise direction with a mortar and pestle.

02 As you do so, programme the herbs by telling them to guide you and ask them to assist the Universe in making the signs a little louder, to guide you along your path.

03 Follow the hot charcoal guide on page 20 to create your spell.

FIRST QUARTER

As the moon grows a little bigger it's time to focus on personal development. Take time to nurture yourself, treat yourself. Ensure you eat only the best food, nourish yourself inside and out. Take note, what is it that can help you grow?

Use this moon power to show the Universe how much you care for and honour yourself. Practise self-care rituals. Look in the mirror and stare deep into your eyes, remind yourself that you are enough.

Celebrate yourself around this time, create yourself a personal power affirmation for the rest of the cycle (see pages 187–189 for affirmations) make a sigil out of the affirmation (see pages 114–115).

PERSONAL POWER POTION

> YOU WILL NEED:
>
> - *5 cloves*
> - *1 pinch of thyme*
> - *1 bay leaf (with a sigil on it for super-power, see pages 114–115)*
> - *5 drops of patchouli essential oil*
> - *a mortar and pestle*

01 First, blend all the dry ingredients with a mortar and pestle to a fine powder.

02 Next, add the patchouli oil and blend in a clockwise direction into a paste.

03 Follow the hot charcoal guide on page 20 to create your spell.

WAXING GIBBOUS

As the moon is almost full, this is a time to revisit your intentions, read them out loud to the moon and restate them. Know that as the moon is growing so are the seeds you have planted.

Take note around this time of any alignments and synchronicities that have been taking place. If you have been facing hurdles to any of your manifestations coming to fruition, this is the time to call in on the Universe and ask to be sent a sign. Ask out loud and then keep your eyes peeled and your ears open. Be open around this time and use these signs to motivate and remind you that your magic is working. This spell calls on the Universe to make the signs a little bit more obvious.

SYNCHRONICITY SPELL

YOU WILL NEED:

- *1 pinch of frankincense*
- *1 star anise*
- *2 pinches of dried rosemary*
- *a mortar and pestle*

01 Blend these ingredients to a fine powder in a clockwise direction with a mortar and pestle.

02 As you do so, programme the herbs by telling them to guide you and ask them to assist the Universe in making the signs a little louder, to guide you along your path.

03 Follow the hot charcoal guide on page 20 to create your spell.

FULL MOON

When the moon is full it is at its most powerful. This high-powered energy has a tendency to create heightened emotions and make us feel a little out of control.

A full moon can often shine light on hidden emotions or fears, or awaken problems we may have tried to bury deep in our shadow side. Scary as this sounds, a full moon is to be embraced, and if you are losing control of your emotions around this time and find yourself going a little crazy, or realise that you can't get to sleep, remind yourself that this means you are connected! This is energy to be harnessed for something positive.

Imagine she is a giant disco ball in the sky and put on your favourite song and dance in the moonlight. Take this time to gaze and moon bathe in the beauty of her glow. Hold your hands up to her and feel her energy wash all over you.

Write out your intentions and bless them in the moonlight. Lay out your crystals and charge them with this magical moon energy.

CONNECTION AND HONOURING SPELL

YOU WILL NEED:

- *3 pinches of sandalwood*
- *1 pinch of ground cinnamon*
- *1 pinch of thyme*
- *1 pinch of dried rose petals*
- *a mortar and pestle*

01 Blend the ingredients to a fine powder, in a clockwise direction with a mortar and pestle.

02 As you do so, thank the moon for her light and energy, and for shining her light on everything that you need to see. This is a great time for manifesting and expressing gratitude for all the things you are happy about in your life.

03 Follow the hot charcoal guide on page 20 to create your spell. Use this smoke to connect to the moon.

WANING GIBBOUS

After the full moon phase the moon starts slightly decreasing and as it does we can take a big, long, relaxing exhale. Ahhhhhhhhhhhhhhhhhhh.

Now that the full charge and intensity of the full moon has passed, these next weeks can be spent taking a little downtime. While relaxing, this is a good time to think about anything that might have come up emotionally for you when the moon was full. She has a habit of shining her light on your emotional triggers – was something revealed around this time?

Use this energy to focus on how you can work with it. Did something come up that you are ready to banish and move on from?

Remember, the unveiling of these feelings or negative traits that we have within ourselves over a full moon is powerful.

BANISHING SPELL

YOU WILL NEED:
• table salt
• 5 black peppercorns
• skin from a garlic bulb
• a pinch of dried sage
• a pinch of dried rosemary
• 10 drops of peppermint oil
• a mortar and pestle
• pen and paper (black ink)
• 1 black candle
• a cauldron or fire-proof pot

01 Create a circle of salt on the floor around you so that you are protected.

02 Blend the peppercorns, garlic bulb skin, sage, rosemary and peppermint oil in a mortar and pestle, in a clockwise direction.

03 Write out whatever it is you want to remove from your life on the paper and light the candle.

04 Scatter the herb mix over the paper, rubbing it on the paper in an anti-clockwise direction. Fold the paper in half (facing away from you) and seal it using the black candle wax. When it is sealed, place it in the cauldron and set fire to it.

05 Sweep up the salt and dispose of it, along with the ashes, far away from your house, or in someone else's bin (or flush them down the toilet).

THIRD QUARTER

During this transitional time of the moon's cycle she is half light and half dark.

This is a time to connect with the transitions you are making or want to make. These may be in your relationships, your living situation or your work-life. Are you finding balance in these places? Do you have healthy boundaries in place? Are you saying 'yes' to too many things? Or maybe you are saying 'no' too much?

BALANCING SPELL

YOU WILL NEED:

- *2 pieces of paper and a pen*
- *2 pinches of benzoin*
- *1 pinch of dried lavender*
- *1 bay leaf*
- *a mortar and pestle*

---

01 Start by making a pie chart and divide it into four parts:

Me – how much time do you spend doing nice things for yourself? This includes reading, getting out in nature, hobbies, daydreaming, resting and relaxing.

Work – how much time you spend at work, thinking about it, preparing work stuff?

Relationships – how much time do you spend with friends and family?

Spirituality – what are you putting out to the Universe? Magic? Spiritual practices? Helping others?

Notice which areas need balancing.

02 Next, blend your ingredients clockwise in a mortar and pestle.

03 Burn this spell (follow the hot charcoal guide on page 20) and draw a second chart, this time creating a more balanced chart that suits your needs.

04 Allow the smoke to work as a reset button to clear out old habits and restore balance in your life. Bless the new chart with the smoke and pin your chart up somewhere so you can see it everyday.

Top Tip: Triple the ingredients of this spell and burn a small amount of it everyday to remind you that you are now choosing a more balanced path.

WANING CRESCENT

This moon phase is the time to declutter your outside world and your inside world. It might be your inbox, your fridge, stuff you haven't used in months that you are hoarding under your bed, or maybe its feelings and emotions, harboured resentments, stuff that has been irritating you, or bad habits (this can include ex-partners or people that you wish to move on from).

Use this time to say goodbye to what is holding you back and no longer serving you and cut the cords.

EMOTIONAL CORD-CUTTER SPELL

YOU WILL NEED:

- *2 pieces of paper (or a photograph of yourself)*
- *a piece of string*
- *1 pinch of rosemary*
- *2 pinches of copal resin*
- *1 black candle*

01 Write your name on one of the pieces of paper or use a photograph of yourself, roll it up and tie the string around it.

02 On the other piece of paper write down what you wish to say goodbye to, roll it up and tie the other end of the string around it.

03 Blend the rosemary and copal and burn it following the hot charcoal guide on page 20.

04 Hold the string over the smoke and cut it in the middle.

05 Burn the paper and the string of what you are saying goodbye to over the black candle.

06 Flush the ashes down the toilet or place them in a bag outside and away from your house.

07 Burn the black candle all the way down to seal the spell.

DARK MOON

This is a time for banishing what you no longer want in your life. Emotions that are holding you back, negative thought patterns, bad energy, a bad lover, a bad habit, boundaries that you feel are being crossed – whatever keeps you up at night worrying.

This is the time to say goodbye. Anything that is not serving you can be banished on this night. It's time to say goodbye so that you can emerge like a new moon butterfly.

RELAXING BATH SALTS

YOU WILL NEED:
• *1 strong cup of chamomile tea* • *9 drops rose essential oil* • *juice 1 lemon* • *a bowl* • *275 g (10 oz/1 cup) of salt*

01 Put the tea, rose oil, and lemon juice in a bowl, then add the salt.

02 Run a bath and add the blend into the running water.

03 Immerse yourself in the water and connect with the releasing energy. This is a time to acknowledge any fears or feelings that are are no longer serving you.

FOLLOW THE MOON FOR SUPERCHARGED MAGIC

ASTROLOGICAL MOON RITUALS

When the moon is full, she is like a battery charged to capacity. There is plenty of power to harness around this time. Yes, we may feel like emotional wrecks and like we are in Luna-tic mode, but it is important to try and zone in on this being a positive sign. Focus on the fact that you are feeling a little high or on edge because you are connected and that you are feeling this way because you are tuning into her almighty frequencies.

How you work with this part of the cycle should be totally intuitive and you should do whatever feels right.

You are free to choose whichever spells feel right on the night, or for a little guidance you can choose to work with astrological alignment.

The full moon in an astrological sign can highlight which areas and energies to focus on to make the most of this effective time, so soak up and harness her energy to amplify any spell-work. As it will be a different sign each month, check online at the time to see where this is falling.

If you don't feel like howling at this time, you may choose to look at this phase as the completion of the cycle and want to relax and review how things have manifested since intentions were set and plants were seeded on the new moon.

ARIES

An Aries full moon has a tendency to shine its light on our impulsive side. Frustrations might show up in the form of extreme reactions. These feelings of annoyance are here to highlight and show you that it is time to take control.

Check in with any energy blocks – is there something or someone that is holding you back? What is it that you need to move on from? Is there something that you are scared of? This is the time to overcome these fears and stand up to them.

This Aries full moon energy is here to assist and motivate you – so use it to call in some assertiveness and take action.

It's time to take note of all the wisdom you have earned and use it to harness your personal power!

FOR THIS PERSONAL POWER SPELL YOU WILL NEED:

- *a black candle*
- *a pen or pencil*
- *a piece of paper*
- *a pinch of cloves (or a few drops of clove oil)*
- *a pinch of dried thyme*
- *a mortar and pestle*

Start by writing out your fears and what no longer serves you, or what you want to break away from on the piece of paper and burn it with the black candle. Say goodbye to it.

Then blend the thyme and cloves using a mortar and pestle, stirring in a clockwise direction and repeat the words 'I am in control of my personal power.' (If you want to add superpower to this spell, write this up and make a sigil see pages 114–115) and then follow the hot charcoal guide on page 20.

TAURUS

A Taurus full moon can awaken the pleasure-seeker within. The lumination of this moon may show up and highlight how self-indulgent you have been – whether it's been shopping sprees, big nights out or being emotionally demanding, or obsessing over things that you don't need to worry about.

This Taurus moon is here to teach you to ground yourself. Don't focus on material things. Get outdoors and align yourself with nature – hug a tree, feed some birds, moon-bathe, and take time to remind yourself how magic is all around us. Nature can feed all of our senses, and connecting with the elements around us is priceless.

FOR THIS GROUNDING SPELL YOU WILL NEED:

- *10 drops of sandalwood essential oil*
- *10 drops of lavender essential oil*
- *10 drops of orange essential oil*
- *20 ml (1 fl oz) of a carrier oil of your choice (almond, coconut, jojoba)*
- *a glass vessel/mason jar/bottle*

Blend the oils in the glass jar and leave it beneath the full moon to soak up the powerful moon energy. Each time you apply the oil repeat the mantra 'I am enough and I get better every day.'

Set an intention that while this full moon energy is in the air you will take yourself somewhere to be surrounded by nature, and apply your oil and repeat your mantra and show gratitude to Mother Earth.

GEMINI

Call in on a Gemini full moon for connections. This may come in as a connection with yourself. Is there something that you are being indecisive about? Use this Gemini moon to help guide you through confusion.

A Gemini full moon also offers a time to recognise how growth can be made within relationships that feature in your life – friends, lovers, family members, pets.

Who do you want to expand your relationship with on this full moon? Beneath this full moon, take the time to write this person (or yourself) a letter of gratitude, letting them know how much you appreciate them and how they have helped you grow.

FOR THIS CONNECTION SPELL YOU WILL NEED:

- *a pinch of sandalwood*
- *a pinch of cinnamon*
- *a bay leaf*
- *a mortar and pestle*

Blend the sandalwood and herbs in a clockwise direction with a mortar and pestle. Burn the mix following the hot charcoal guide on page 20.

As this incense burns, tell the smoke all of the things that you have gratitude for and ask it to send blessings and good vibes to all of those who you love and cherish. If you are calling in friends, try a mantra such as 'my vibe attracts my tribe'.

CANCER

A Cancer full moon will shine light on your nurturing side. You may feel the urge, under the energy of this full moon, to nest and embrace your maternal side. This could come up by looking at how you care for yourself or how you look after others. Perhaps under this full moon you may feel a deeper empathy for people around you, or a new-found compassion for yourself, which might bring up emotions that you have been hoarding from deep in your subconscious.

Check in around this time and recognise how you talk to yourself, is your inner voice being nurturing around this time?

MOON MILK RECIPE – COOKING WITH THE INTENTION OF LOVE
YOU WILL NEED:

- 500 ml (17 fl oz/2 cups) of nut milk of your choice, warmed
- ½ teaspoon ground cardamom
- 2 teaspoons agave syrup
- a few drops of rose water

Blend the ingredients a little at a time to create a paste. Blend in a clockwise direction and as you do this set the intention of spreading love to yourself and whoever you are making it for. Call in on your spirit guides to send you signs of love – feel them blessing your magical moon milk as you stir it. Drink the milk beneath the full moon, with friends or alone. Send love to yourself, send love to the moon and send love to the Universe.

LEO

A full moon in Leo gives us permission to roar!

Use this moon energy to call in your courage and embrace your inner strength. This is a time for self-empowerment and to celebrate yourself. Be careful around this Leo energy to keep your ego in check – have you been treating those around you with respect and love?

This is a great time to make a courage potion – blessed beneath this moon it is something you can call in on at any time. Use it when you feel the need to tap into some Leo full moon fire-power!

FOR THE POWER POTION
YOU WILL NEED:

- a glass bottle or mason jar
- a pinch of cloves
- a pinch of black pepper
- 10 drops of bergamot essential oil
- 5 drops of thyme essential oil

- *100 ml (3½ fl oz/scant ½ cup) of a carrier oil of your choice (almond, coconut, jojoba)*

Blend the ingredients in the glass bottle, in a clockwise direction, and leave beneath the full moon to soak up the power of the Leo Moon.

Annoint yourself with the oil, wherever you choose, and then give yourself permission to take courage.

VIRGO

The full moon in Virgo is a good time for a little introspection. It can be a good idea during this moon phase to spend a little time on your own, to declutter your mind. You may also choose to have a bit of a clear-out and tidy up your personal space at this time. Removing items that no longer serve you in your life is a great way to shake up stagnant energy – clear out the old to make room for the new. Decluttering will help to bring the clarity that this Virgo moon will urge you to seek.

Beneath this full moon, cleanse yourself inside and out with a tea and a bath.

FOR THE TEA YOU WILL NEED:

This is enough to make one pot:
- *2 pinches of fennel seeds*

- *a few sprigs of fresh mint*
- *half a lemon*

Put the ingredients in a teapot, cover in boiling water and allow to steep for 5 minutes.

As you drink the tea, visualise everything that no longer serves you getting smaller and smaller, until eventually it disappears.

TO CREATE A BATHING RITUAL YOU WILL NEED:

- *275 g (10 oz/2 cups) Epsom salts*
- *5 drops of eucalyptus essential oil*
- *5 drops of lemon essential oil*
- *5 drops of geranium essential oil*

Add the salts and oils to the bath as it fills with water. As you soak in the bath allow yourself to let go of your stresses – let the magical aroma clear your mind and reset your energy. Lie in the bath and follow the steps of the tea visualisation, shrinking what no longer serves you until it vanishes.

LIBRA

If areas of your life are unbalanced, then a Libra full moon will most definitely highlight what's not right. If there has been any conflict in your life, this is a time to make peace with it – forgive and move on. Any negative energy, anger or resentment that you are hoarding will be weighing you down even more right now. It is blocking the abundance that could be flowing to you.

This is a time to send healing and bright white light to whatever is bugging you.

Remember whatever has annoyed you and wound you up should not be your priority. Focus on healing and restoring yourself on this full moon. Once this situation is fixed, your manifestations will flow freely.

TO BANISH THIS NEGATIVE ENERGY YOU WILL NEED:

- *a pen or pencil*
- *a piece of paper*
- *the papery white skin of a garlic bulb*
- *a pinch of black pepper*
- *a pinch of sage*
- *a mortar and pestle*
- *a cauldron or fireproof pot to burn everything in*

Start by writing a goodbye letter to whatever this negative energy is – tell it that it is no longer welcome in your life. When you have written it, fold the paper away from you in an anti-clockwise direction, and fold it away from you three times.

Then blend the garlic skin, pepper and sage using a mortar and pestle in an anti-clockwise direction. As you blend, imagine the face of the person or the situation you are banishing moving further and further away from you. Imagine it getting smaller and smaller.

Light the paper and place it in the cauldron and then add the spell mix over the flames. Allow the whole piece of paper and all of the mix to burn. As everything is burning, say goodbye, and know that you have moved on and this problem will no longer haunt you.

SCORPIO

A Scorpio full moon can highlight sensitivities and take you on a journey deep down to the depths of your emotions. When visiting these depths during a Scorpio full moon, it is a time to tap into your intuition. Observe what's coming up, harness this energy to help you get answers. If you have been ignoring any emotions, you won't be able to hide from them at this time – what are the blocks that you are feeling? Are there any limiting beliefs that are stopping you from being able to scream your heart's desires at the top of your voice? Have you been ignoring emotions? If so, this is a time to release them and connect to your passions.

TO RELEASE ANY NEGATIVE EMOTIONS YOU WILL NEED:

- *a pen or pencil*
- *a piece of paper*
- *a black candle*

Write a goodbye letter to any emotions and setbacks that have no place in your life. Fold the piece of paper away from you in an anti-clockwise direction and burn it over a black candle.

FOR THE SCORPIO PASSION POTION YOU WILL NEED:

- *10 drops of patchouli essential oil*
- *5 drops of sandalwood essential oil*
- *5 drops of benzoin*
- *1 stick of cinnamon*
- *100 ml of a carrier oil of your choice (almond, coconut, jojoba)*
- *a mortar and pestle*

Blend the ingredients with a mortar and pestle in a clockwise direction and leave beneath the full moon to soak up the powerful moon energy. Use this oil as a perfume and use it to anoint anything you want to add passion to.

SAGITTARIUS

When a full moon is in Sagittarius it is likely that it might have you wondering what your life purpose is and you may find yourself questioning your destiny. This moon has a habit of inspiring holidays, travel and adventures.

It is a time for growth and expansion. Allow this moon to remind you that it isn't so important to always be right. When you let go of certain beliefs, things can just fall into place and the greatest energy shifts happen. When the Universe sees us let go it has a knack of sending opportunities our way.

Use this spell to open your mind and the road ahead.

FOR THE ROAD-OPENING SPELL YOU WILL NEED:

- *a pinch of dried rosemary*
- *a pinch of thyme*
- *a pinch of peppermint*
- *a mortar and pestle*

Blend the ingredients with a mortar and pestle, in a clockwise direction, asking for the spell to open doors and guide you. Burn the spell mix following the hot charcoal guide on page 20. Save the burnt charcoal and on the next new moon dispose of it at a crossroads (see page 21).

CAPRICORN

Capricorn's energy brings with it a 'taking care of business' attitude! Call in on all things practical right now – make a list of all your career achievements and give yourself recognition for all of your efforts and goals reached. Celebrate your success and then make a list of all of your career goals. What do you wish to achieve over the year ahead? Write out a list and think big!

There couldn't be a better moon to lay down foundations and set intentions for all of the success you want to call into your life.

This is a 'get up and go' spell to get you motivated to start reaching those goals.

YOU WILL NEED:

- *5 pinches of rosemary*
- *2 pinches of lemongrass (or 10 drops of lemongrass essential oil)*
- *1 pinch of galangal*

Blend the ingredients in a clockwise direction. As you do this, think of all of your upcoming goals and know that this potion is going to give you the power and courage to get out there and achieve all of the amazing things that are on your list. Leave out beneath the full moon to soak up the full moon energy.

Burn the spell mix following the hot charcoal guide on page 20 for motivation to reach your goals. Burn this before you start work in the morning and visualise achieving all of your goals as you watch the smoke rise.

AQUARIUS

The Aquarius full-moon energy is here to expect the unexpected – so if ever there was a time to experiment and try out something new, now would be the time to do it! Harness this moon-power to go for it and banish your fears. Don't hold back, put yourself out there, this is a time to shake stuff up! It might be starting a course, some form of exercise or starting a new creative project. You know deep down what this is meant to be and this is the time to do it!

FOR THIS REVEALING SPELL YOU WILL NEED:

- *a pinch of frankincense resin*
- *a pinch of sandalwood*
- *a pinch of cedarwood*
- *a mortar and pestle*
- *a pen or pencil*
- *a piece of paper*

Blend the frankincense, sandalwood and cedarwood with a mortar and pestle in a clockwise direction. As you do so, ask the spell mix to guide you and give you the answers you seek.

Burn the spell mix following the hot charcoal guide on page 20, and as the smoke travels up, close your eyes and write. Write whatever comes to mind – ask the Universe to show you the way, know that the smoke will assist you with writing out what you are meant to do.

PISCES

Emotions run high during a Pisces full moon. When water signs are passing through it can really feel like the tide is high, but hang in there and sit with your emotions. Release what no longer serves you. This is the time to recognise that you are worthy of good things.

FULL MOON WATER SPELL
YOU WILL NEED:

- *a glass bottle or mason jar*
- *a black marker pen*
- *a label (optional)*
- *water*

Create your own sigil (see pages 114–115). Draw your sigil on a label or,

even better, directly on a glass bottle or mason jar. Fill the bottle with water and leave it out beneath the full Pisces moon to soak up all of that full-moon energy. Drink the water at sunrise the following day, repeating the mantra 'I am worthy of good things.'

CRYSTAL ENERGY

Crystals are, quite simply, gifts from Mother Earth. They are minerals that form underground, and as they grow they connect with different energetic properties and elements from the Earth's core. Their unique structures, colours and shapes have different meanings, and each carry their own magical vibrations.

INTRODUCTION

The way I look at crystals is that they are friends. Just as in your close-knit group, you have your favourite crystals.

One of my favourite crystals of all time was called Charmaine; she was of a substantial size, about half the size of my palm, a rose quartz, and she was unpolished. As attached as you might get to your crystals, remember that once they have served their purpose, they will find a way to leave you – whether that is getting themselves lost, or giving a sign that they should be gifted to someone else in need. Charmaine came into my life when I had faced really big heartache; she was always in my bag, no matter how small it was. I knew that she was there to remind me that I was worthy of love, and

not to forget self-care. She inspired the self-love spell that I use in all my rituals today. I lost her around the time that I found the love of my life. I took her to guided meditations with me, to Bali, to Stonehenge and to many a spring and autumn equinox – she was even washed in the white well in Glastonbury. It's safe to say that she really lived a life; when I think back about her, I remember every ridge and rough edge, and how she felt in my hand. I have no idea where she is now, but I like to think that whoever she is with is receiving the same support and guidance that she gave me. I hope that sharing this story shows you just how deep a connection you can have with your crystals, and that quality and connection are far more important than quantity.

At the moment, there are a lot of reports of immoral practices when it comes to crystal-mining. As crystals gain popularity, the demand for them becomes so much greater, and sadly this complicates the way they are being sourced. It's very important to be aware of their provenance, and know where they have come from. As tempting as it is to keep adding to your collection, remember that you only need a few star players.

HOW TO GIVE YOUR CRYSTALS A HOME

Really try to go with what you feel here; connect with the crystal and allow it to guide you as to how to store it. These are a few places that I store my crystals:

- On the windowsill to call in the energy that you are working with.

- Buried in your front garden or in a pot outside the door for protection.

- In your bag, bra or pockets to keep close to you – what did you think that small pocket in your jeans was for?

- On your bedside table, but this will take some experimentation, as some crystals radiate too much energy and may interupt a good night's sleep.

- In charm bags with corresponding herbs to keep them activated (see page 33).

CRYSTAL

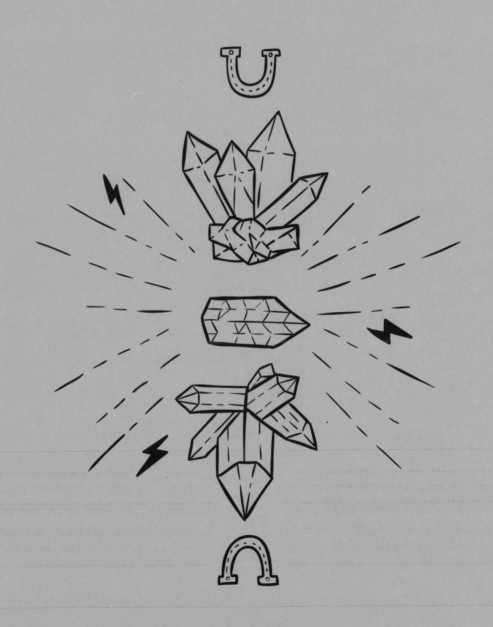

ACTIVATION

CRYSTALS FOR ABUNDANCE AND PROSPERITY

The herbs to bless these crystals will bring positivity around wealth, courage for you push your business and promote yourself, and luck to call in abundance.

AMANZONITE — Luck, inspiration, brings new business opportunities

GREEN AVENTURINE — Inspires creativity, confidence to go and get what you want in the world

EMERALD — Brings in luck, opens up the heart chakra to receive abundance

PROSPERITY SPELL

YOU WILL NEED:

- a pinch of basil
- 2 pinches of patchouli
- a pinch of sandalwood (to add extra oooomph to this spell add a bay leaf with a sigil on it – see pages 114–115)

01 Blend the herbs in a clockwise direction in a mortar and pestle, telling them what you want them to bring you (follow the hot charcoal guide on page 20).

02 Bathe the crystal of your choice in the magical smoke and say what this crystal has helped with... say it like it's already happened, know that you are giving this crystal a message of what it has to do for you.

03 Keep it with you at all times; it will work as a magnet attracting all that you have programmed it with.

CRYSTALS FOR PROTECTION

BLACK TOURMALINE	AKA The Bodyguard
BLUE KYANITE	Creates boundaries, wards off bullies and narcissists
BLACK OBSIDIAN	Breaks hexes and curses, sends back any negative energy that has been sent to you

PROTECTION SPELL

YOU WILL NEED:

- *3 pinches of rosemary*
- *1 pinch of frankincense*
- *7 drops of angelica root essential oil*

01 Blend the ingredients in a clockwise direction in a mortar and pestle. As you do so call in on their powers asking them to bring you protection and to take care of you.

02 Imagine your ideal bodyguard, call in on your guardians to bless the spell, as you blend feel their energy surround you with love and know these vibes that you are feeling are being added to your spell as you blend it. Burn over charcoal, following the hot charcoal guide on page 20.

03 As the spell burns, bathe your crystals in the smoke and watch them soak up the protective energy, and know that your guides have added their power to the smoke to shield you from negative energy to keep you safe.

04 Keep the crystals by your front door or in your pocket, bra or bag to ensure protection at all times.

CRYSTALS FOR HEALING AND GROUNDING

APACHE TEARS	Helps to relieve grief (good for grieving animals too). Brings harmony to tense situations
AMETHYST	AKA The carer. This crystal protects and is the ultimate stress reliever
SMOKEY QUARTZ	Helps with anxiety, can calm your mood and bring calm to a stressful environment

GROUNDING SPELL

YOU WILL NEED:

- *2 pinches of lavender*
- *1 pinch of cinnamon*
- *2 pinches of myrrh*

01 As you blend these herbs visualise yourself in your favourite safe place: this could be somewhere in your home, a particular holiday, or somewhere in nature, or even a time when you were feeling really good within yourself. As you blend the herbs, close your eyes and take yourself to this safe place, feel it, notice how it makes your body feel, can you remember any sensations it brings? Feel them all and imagine these safe feelings and sensations bringing their energy through your hand as you stir the spell.

02 When you feel like you have enchanted the spell with your hand start to burn it over the hot charcoal (follow the hot charcoal guide on page 20).

03 Hold your crystal in both hands over the smoke and let them soak up the blessing, feel the energy of your safe place transit through the spell and in to your crystal.

04 Anytime you need to call in on your crystals power, ask it it to release the power of your memory to remind you of your safe and grounded place.

CRYSTALS TO HELP YOU FOCUS AND BRING CLARITY

CARNELIAN   Energise you, banishes self sabotage

TIGERS EYE   Great for creativity and concentration

CITRINE   AKA Mr Motivator

CLARITY SPELL

YOU WILL NEED:

- *a glass jar*
- *100 ml (3½ fl oz/ scant ½ cup) of a carrier oil of your choice*
- *10 drops of lavender essential oil*
- *10 drops of bergamot essential oil*
- *5 drops of lemon essential oil*
- *1 pinch of dried thyme essential oil*

01 Add the carrier oil to the jar first and then, as you add the essential oils, visualise yourself completing tasks and focussed. Hold on to the feeling as your stir the ingredients.

02 Next add the crystals to the jar and leave them in the jar to soak up the energy overnight. Know that they are charged with super focus energy.

03 You can also choose to leave these crystals in the potion and use it as an oil to add to anoint yourself with on days when you need to be totally on it.

CRYSTALS FOR LOVE AND RELATIONSHIPS

ROSE QUARTZ   Rose quartz is the stone of universal love, hold it over your heart to activate your heart chakra and feel love both coming in and going out to the Universe

KUNZITE   Great for opening up your heart to yourself, banishes negative self talk, self love and courage

LAPIS LAZULI   Fantastic for communication and helping you to speak from the heart

LOVE SPELL

YOU WILL NEED:
• 1 pinch of allspice • 2 pinches of roses • 1 pinch of myrrh • 6 drops of patchouli essential oil

01 All love spells should start with love for yourself, a deep unconditional love, that allows to to speak from the heart with a nurturing voice. If you are wanting to attract love ask the crystals to allow you to open your heart.

02 Blend in a clockwise direction with a mortar and pestle and, as you do so, imagine everything that and everyone you love, feel it in your body, keep stirring until you are feeling so much love that your heart is beating a little faster.

03 When you feel the time is right stop stirring and burn over the hot coal (follow the hot charcoal guide on page 20).

04 Hold a crystal in one hand over the smoke and your other hand over your heart. Know that the crystal is soaking up all of this loving energy; take this time to ask the crystal for the kind of love you wish it to provide you with. When you feel that the crystal has understood its purpose, hold it close to your heart and thank it for all the love it will surround you with.

SPIRITUAL

SELF-CARE

LEARNING
TO MANIFEST

Manifesting, in essence, is setting intentions.
It's putting a clear idea of what you want in
your head. You might have vague ideas of
what you wish for in your life, or even what
you don't, but haven't managed to create
a clear focus. Recognising that you are a
co-creator, and have the power to work with
the Universe and have a hand in creating your
realities is at the heart of manifesting.

INTRODUCTION

According to a recent study by Dr Gail Matthews, there is a correlation between achievement and verbalising or writing down your goals. In fact, you are 42 per cent more likely to make your wishes reality if you do write them down, as cited in Mary Morrissey's article in the *Huffington Post*, 'The Power of Writing Down'. That 42 per cent, combined with a little magic, can send intentions into the stratosphere.

HOW TO MAGICALLY MANIFEST

Be clear on what you want – a strong vision of this is imperative. If you are struggling to define this, or need focus, take a sprig of rosemary and rub it on your third eye (see page 65 for Third-eye Chakra). When you are focussing on your vision and what you want to call in, you need to make sure you are in a good head space, and operating from a place of self love, not a place of desperation or darkness. If you are asking for things when you are not feeling 100 per cent, you might not be asking for things that will be good for you.

When the vision is clear, it's totally fine to ask for more material items, but I would suggest that you focus on how you will feel when these things come to fruition – such as a sense of security, contentedness, happiness, love or joy. When you are thinking of these things, really feel these emotions in your body. You've got to know that as co-creator with the Universe, you also have your part to play in making these happen and effort to put in.

If you are looking for love or performing a love spell, or want a new job, you can't expect it to come knocking on your door. You have to work with the Universe and get yourself out there.Always trust in the process of divine timing, it's important to know that sometimes things may not work out in the way that you expected, and know that magic works in mysterious ways. It's also important to always express gratitude to the Universe when your manifesting comes to fruition.

Speaking things into existence

Manifesting doesn't have to be a solo activity. It can be a powerful thing to do with friends. Simply gather around, and talk with each other as if it were six months in the future; speak like you are living in the life that you have manifested. Discuss what it will be like to walk through the door of your home, dating your crush, working in your dream job – let your imagination run wild.

For the best times to call things in, refer to the moon phases that will amplify your manifestations (see pages 72–82).

WAYS TO MAGICALLY MANIFEST

You'll find guidelines on how to manifest by writing a letter to the Universe, vision boarding, calling things in and sigils on the following pages, but, in each instance, remember the following points to make the most of your manifesting moments:

01 **To call things in, you will also need to let things go.** When you release things in your life that are creating negativity and holding you back, you make room for positives. See the ritual on page 91 to find out how to release negative emotions.

02 **Think big** – don't limit yourself.

03 **Be wary when using people's names** – you should only be focussing on yourself when manifesting, and not messing with other people's energy.

04 **If you are feeling stuck or lost**, or your manifestations aren't happening, ask out loud for the Universe to send you signs.

05 Remember that **magic takes patience**.

06 Once manifesting, **be in the headspace of expectation**, knowing that better is on its way to you, in whatever form that takes.

WRITING A LETTER TO THE UNIVERSE

When you write a letter to the Universe it's important to remember to always be grateful; you need to write as if you already have it. As you are writing, feel the excitement and contentment that will be in your life, visualising it flowing from you, through the pen to the paper as you do so.

As well as asking for the big things – the next big job, or a dream holiday – don't forget to ask for smaller treats, which could include anything from a head massage to a new pair of boots. I would recommend signing and dating the letter – it's a crazy but wonderful thing to look back on. Lastly, always end your letter to the Universe with 'this or better', as you don't know what the Universe has in mind for you. You don't want to limit yourself, and the Universe might have bigger ideas for you than you could ever imagine. Yes, you can just write the letter, but the magical super-boost from using attraction oil can't be underestimated.

Remember to start as you mean to go on – that means choosing your favourite stationery, maybe even investing in some special paper. If you need some help getting in the zone, try raising your vibrations (see pages 116–117), and then begin to write. It's as simple as that.

Once you've finished your letter and signed it, anoint it with the attraction oil in a clockwise direction, folding the paper towards you three times, turning it towards you in an clockwise direction with each fold. Keep the paper somewhere safe, and wait for the magic to happen.

YOU WILL NEED:

• *a pen and paper*
• *Attraction oil (see page 136)*

VISION BOARDING

Sometimes when manifesting it's hard to put into words what you want, even if you have a clear image of it. This can often help to develop your visualisation, and connect to what you want on a deeper level. A vision board can come in all shapes and sizes. You could create a scrapbook, cover a cardboard box in cut-outs of images, or just cut and paste and draw your visions on a piece of cardboard. Or, call in on technology and make it the screensaver on your laptop or phone, or even do a Pinterest board. This can be a fun thing to do as a group – invite people over and make a night of it, getting people to bring magazines and newspapers, scissors and glue, and even begin with a tea ceremony (see pages 200–201). Really, cut out anything you are drawn to – buzzwords, positive affirmations, photographs – anything that represents how you want to feel.

To give your vision board extra magical oomph, add sigils (see pages 114–115), attach a pouch of corresponding dried herbs (see pages 42–43), or anoint with attraction oil (see page 136). As a side note, make sure you are 100 per cent happy with the images on your board – you shouldn't see anything that you don't want, or use any pictures of things you don't want in your life.

SIGILS

A sigil is a powerful symbol that you can create and infuse with your energy and intentions. These are great for when you don't have the space or materials to create a full ritual and can they can also be added as a potent addition to spells. All you need is a pen, paper and a statement of intent. The other thing that I love about these sigils is that once you have made one, you can close your eyes and call in on its power anytime wherever you may be, in a similar way to how you may connect with your favourite crystal you can connect with your favourite sigil.

The statements of intent that you can use on a sigil can be of emotional support, reminding you that you are loved and cared for, or they can be used as little life coaches used to cheer you along prompting confidence and courage. You can also use them for straight up manifesting material items and treats. (I once used the power of a sigil to take me away somewhere hot and it brought me an all expenses paid holiday to Bali!)

I have made two here, which you are welcome to connect with and use, but it's worth pointing out that a sigil is always going to be more potent if you create your own.

The first sigil I have created is with the intention to help you surrender. I really wanted to acknowledge the law of attraction here, which states that any negative thoughts or emotions will block good things coming to you – this is quite simply not the case. Sometimes life can throw challenges at you and during these moments it can feel impossible to be happy, celebrate gratitude or even believe that the Universe could put you in such a position. It is important to sometimes sit with these feelings and quite simply, surrender to them. Knowing that it's totally ok to experience all of your emotions, the happy times the sad times and all that comes in between. I made this surrender sigil for myself through a particularly challenging time in my life and I hope it can guide you through as it guided me. Anytime you are feeling like everything is getting a bit too much, just close your eyes and visualise it. Take some deep breaths, visualise and know that whatever feeling you are surrendering to will soon pass.

YOU WILL NEED:

- *a pen and paper*
- *a bay leaf (fresh or dried)*
- *a black marker pen*

The second sigil here is 'I am worthy of good things'. This is a great one to call in on anytime when you wake up in the morning visualise it as you wake up, use it before a job interview, a date, add it to your manifestation lists. Know that there is absolutely no reason why you aren't worthy of good things, and believe it!

01   Firstly, make sure you will have this time to yourself – this isn't something to be rushed. Light some candles or incense, make a cup of tea, or whatever else feels right. Think of your intention statement; it should begin with 'I am', 'I will' or 'I have'. Once you've established what it is, write it out then cross out all of the vowels, then cross out any of the consonants that have been repeated, therefore, only leaving one of each consonant.

02   Next, use these letters to create a symbol on the page, below your mission statement. I can't stress how important it is to play here; turn your 'r' upside down, lose a curve from your 's', allow your 't' to be a dot, even turn it into a doodle – there are no rules here. Keep repeating your mission statement as you do this, either out loud or in your head. As you are doing this, you are creating a very powerful magical symbol – you might feel hyped-up, similar to a caffeine buzz. Use this excitement to embrace the energy of your symbol.

03   When you are happy with your symbol, step away from it for a little while – this can be anything from 30 minutes to a day, whatever feels comfortable to you. Just make sure that in this period you have clearly memorised the symbol, and that your connection is maintained.

04   At this stage, draw your symbol on a bay leaf with your black marker. You then need to connect your energy with it.

This can be done in a number of ways – emotionally, energetically and sexually – the idea is to get your body in a different energetic state, and charge your sigil with a part of yourself. If you are feeling extreme emotion, either tears of joy or tears of sadness, bless your sigil on the bay leaf with your tears. To do so energetically, put on your favourite song and dance, as vibrantly as you can, getting your heart beating fast, like a high-vibing being, and then, when you can't dance anymore, bless it with your saliva. Finally, my favourite and most powerful way, is to use your sexual energy. Masturbate, and then as you are about to reach orgasm, visualise your symbol, then use your body's fluid to bless the sigil. Once you have blessed the sigil, burn the bay leaf and know that whatever you have manifested will be coming to you. You've set that spell out free into the Universe, and any time you need to call on this just close your eyes and visualise. This symbol can stay with you forever – you might find yourself drawing it in the sand on a beach, in the steamed glass of the shower... anywhere.

STRENGTHENING YOUR POWERS AND RAISING YOUR VIBRATIONS

We are all cosmic beings, connected by unseen energy and magical vibrations that surround us. As our hearts beat they create an electromagnetic field that can be detected up to two metres (six feet) away from the body in all directions. This divine and unseen electromagnetic life-force energy field is something we can tune into at any time. It is a powerful way to raise your vibrations, strengthen your inner super-powers and maximise your magic... fast!

Before maximising your power to this level and working with life-force energy, it is important to be in the right head-space. Are you operating from a place of love? Always remember that when you are operating from a place of love for yourself and others, you can be sure that you will always be sourcing the best possible outcome for everyone.

Ensure that you have given yourself enough time so you don't feel rushed and you can truly focus. It is important to feel grounded and in your body when raising your vibrations.

I would also suggest switching off from all technology devices for as long as you can for maximum impact.

01

- Start by placing your less dominant hand on your heart and then place your leading hand on top of that hand.

- Close your eyes and feel your heartbeat.

- Take a few deep breaths, inhale and exhale slowly and gently.

- Think of someone you love (a human or an animal).

- Feel all of the love that you feel for them.

- Focus on how much you care for them.

- Feel your heart energy connect to their heart energy.

- Visualise the beams transmitting from your heart to theirs and their heart to yours.

- Sit with that feeling, feel your hearts connect and smile!

- When the time feels right open your eyes.

- Take a few deep breaths!

02

- Again, place your less dominant hand on your heart and then place your leading hand on top of that hand.

- Close your eyes and feel your heartbeat.

- Take a few slow, long and deep breaths.

- Now, think of something that excites you? Something that turns you on?

- Focus on what gets your juices flowing.

- Take some time visualising it.

- Continue imagining it until you can feel your body tingling with it.

- Once you can feel this energy, connect it with a colour.

- Then imagine this colour as a bright light beaming out of your body.

- Connect with your heart, which may be beating a little faster now, and this life force energy being transmitted out of your body.

- Visualise this light blessing you and your magic.

- Feel it working as a powerful magnet to draw what you are calling in.

- Know that this energy is being sent out and received by the Universe.

- When you feel ready, open your eyes – you will probably be feeling a magical buzz right now.

- Enjoy the feeling and know that you can tap into this energy any time, simply by reminding yourself of the colour that you associate with this feeling.

- Use this high-vibing moment to blend potions, perform spells and write out your intentions.

LOTIONS AND POTIONS

Scent magic is my favourite type of magic because not only do all the herbs and flowers contain magical properties, scent is also linked to science and the limbic system.

When I was at university studying psychology, I learned that smell becomes ingrained in our lineage; experiments have been done that prove reactions to scent can be passed on through generations. Scent has so many functions; it can inspire, relax and even motivate you in the right strengths and combinations. The following potions are a way of incorporating magic into your daily life, whether by using a body scrub in the shower first thing, or using a vaporiser mix to bring abundance into your home.

BODY SCRUBS

01 In an airtight container, mix all the ingredients together until well incorporated.

02 As you mix, stir in a clockwise direction, focussing on the kind of boost in energy you need as you do so (this will depend on which of the scrubs you are making).

03 Once mixed, put the lid on the container and keep in the shower to use when you want them. Think again of your intention as you lightly massage the scrub over your skin before rinsing.

TO INVIGORATE AND INSPIRE
YOU WILL NEED:

- *275 g (10 oz/1 cup) of salt (sea salt or something very coarse is best)*
- *125 ml (4½ fl oz/½ cup) carrier oil of your choice (almond, coconut, jojoba)*
- *10 drops of bergamot essential oil*
- *5 drops of thyme essential oil*

TO RELEASE AND RENEW
YOU WILL NEED:

- *275 g (10 oz/1 cup) of salt (sea salt or something very coarse is best)*
- *125 ml (4½ fl oz/½ cup) carrier oil of your choice (almond, coconut, jojoba)*
- *5 drops of sage essential oil*
- *6 drops of mint essential oil*
- *5 drops of rosemary essential oil*

BATH OILS

01 In a glass bottle with an airtight lid, mix all the oils together. As you do so, think of the intention that you wish to fill your bath oil with.

02 Replace the lid then add to your bath water as and when needed. Think of the intention that your bath oil will be boosting, then sit back and relax!

TO INVIGORATE AND ACTIVATE YOU WILL NEED:

- *20 drops of thyme essential oil*
- *5 drops of frankincense essential oil*
- *5 drops of grapefruit essential oil*
- *200 ml (7 fl oz/scant 1 cup) of a carrier oil (almond, coconut, jojoba)*

TO SOOTHE AND CALM YOU WILL NEED:

- *10 drops of lavender essential oil*
- *5 drops of rose essential oil*
- *5 drops of sandalwood essential oil*
- *200 ml (7 fl oz/scant 1 cup) of a carrier oil (almond, coconut, jojoba)*

BODY OILS

01 In a glass bottle with an airtight lid, mix all the oils together. As you do so, think of the intention that you wish to fill your body oil with.

02 Replace the lid then use to massage or moisturise your skin as and when you need it. Think of the intention behind the potion as you do so to charge with cosmic energy.

COSMIC CUDDLE
YOU WILL NEED:

- *15 drops of lavender essential oil*
- *8 drops of vanilla extract*
- *100 ml (3½ fl oz/scant ½ cup) of a carrier oil (almond, coconut, jojoba)*

POWER POTION
YOU WILL NEED:

- *10 drops of rose essential oil*
- *5 drops of sandalwood essential oil*
- *5 drops of patchouli essential oil*

VAPOURISER MIXES

01 Mix the ingredients together, focussing on your intention, depending on your chosen vapouriser mix.

02 Add the mix to your vapouriser, following the manufacturer's instructions, or pour into a spray bottle. As the mix fills the air, remind yourself of the intention for the day.

TO WELCOME ABUNDANCE
YOU WILL NEED:

- *3 drops of orange essential oil*
- *3 drops of patchouli essential oil*
- *2 drops of cinnamon essential oil*

Or to make in a spray bottle:
- *100 ml (3½ fl oz) spray bottle*
- *80 ml (2½ fl oz) distilled water*
- *20 ml (1 fl oz) vodka (or witch hazel)*
- *8 drops of orange essential oil*
- *8 drops of patchouli essential oil*
- *4 drops of cinnamon essential oil*

FOR HEALING ENERGY
YOU WILL NEED:

- *2 drops of peppermint essential oil*
- *3 drops of lavender essential oil*
- *3 drops of frankincense essential oil*

Or to make in a spray bottle:
- *100 ml (3½ fl oz) spray bottle*
- *80 ml (2½ fl oz) distilled water*
- *20 ml (1 fl oz) vodka (or witch hazel)*
- *4 drops of peppermint essential oil*
- *8 drops of lavender essential oil*
- *8 drops of frankincense essential oil*

DAILY
CHALLENGES

It only takes a little bit of cosmic
consciousness to tune in and notice
that there is magic in everything.
Your thoughts, your words and your
action carry magical energy and
can bring magical vibes to your
life everyday.

INTRODUCTION

A daily ritual is a great way of getting back in touch with yourself; you can even make the mundane magic – it's all about having a cosmic consciousness of everything that you do. In essence, this is taking a moment each day to check-in and incorporate self-love into your routine. This can be anything from taking the time to cook and enjoy a tasty dinner, going to see some art or a film or taking a walk through the park. It's important to remember that not all rituals need to include magic, crystals and candles – the magic is within you. For instance, if something has been troubling you and you haven't been able to make a decision, you can go for a walk with an intention – asking the Universe to show you signs, knowing that by the time you've made it around the block, what you've asked will have become clearer.

Each day has a magical correspondence with an element of our solar system, which can add super-power to your rituals. The chart opposite explains the relevance of each.

DAY	ELEMENT	CORRESPONDENCE	COLOURS	HERBS AND SPICES	CRYSTAL
Monday	The Moon	• Nurturing • Emotions • Intuition • Divination	Silver	• Chamomile • Myrrh • Sage • Sandalwood	Moonstone
Tuesday	Mars	• Releasing • Breakthroughs • Courage • Will-power	Red	• Dragon's blood • Pepper • Ginger • Basil	Carnelian
Wednesday	Mercury	• Communication • New ideas • Insights	Violet	• Frankincense • Lavender • Thyme	Opal
Thursday	Jupiter	• Abundance • Luck • Business • Learning	Purple	• Patchouli • Cloves • Cedar	Amethyst
Friday	Venus	• Pleasure • Love • Self-love • Friendship	Green	• Cardamom • Rose • Saffron • Sandalwood	Rose quartz
Saturday	Saturn	• Spirituality • Overcoming obstacles • Healing	Blue	• Lavender • Cinnamon	Sapphire
Sunday	The Sun	• Personal achievement • Friendship • Gratitude	Gold	• Cedar • Cinnamon • Frankincense • Lemon	Topaz

You can use this as a guide to help you harness the energy that each day of the week brings. However, it's equally important to follow your intuition, so if you feel you want to wear gold on a Wednesday, go for it.

THE SEVEN-DAY RITUAL CHALLENGE

This is a structured way of getting into the habit of creating a little magic for yourself every day. I would suggest gathering your tools on Saturday so you can begin your challenge on Sunday – see this as a cosmic contract with yourself for the week ahead. But you can mix this up depending on your intuition, and your schedule – the emphasis here is on intention, not rigidity. Even one ritual per week is an achievement – remember the Universe loves it when you do kind things for yourself.

SUNDAY

On this day, let the sun shine on your personal achievements of the past week. This is a day to celebrate, and give yourself a pat on the back. If the sun is shining bright, it's also a day to gather with friends.

YOU WILL NEED:

- *7 small strips of paper*
- *a pen*
- *a Mason jar*
- *2–3 cinnamon sticks*
- *a pinch of patchouli*
- *a magnet or lodestone crystal*

The challenge:
On each piece of paper, write down something that has made you happy over the past week; this is the time to celebrate anything and everything, from seeing a cute dog in the park and treating yourself to a cup of coffee on your commute to taking an afternoon nap.

Fold the papers up, put them in the jar with the cinnamon sticks, patchouli and magnet, then place the jar on a windowsill that gets plenty of sunlight. Add to the jar as and when, or try to make it a Sunday ritual. The cinnamon brings your happiness blessings, and the magnet and patchouli draw many more of these good things to you.

MONDAY

This day is all about inner work; tapping into your intuition, and a great day to give yourself a tea leaf reading (see pages 170–177). Doing inner work also means nourishing your body, which is the focus of today's ritual.

The challenge:

Cook yourself something seasonal and delicious that makes you feel nourished, both inside and out. As you are cooking, consciously stir and blend your ingredients in a clockwise direction, putting your intention into your food. Repeat the mantra 'everything always works out for me', or, if you are cooking for friends 'Everything always works out for us, and everyone that I love'.

TUESDAY

Mars rules on this day – powering emotional and creative breakthroughs. This is the time to surrender and release what is no longer serving you. You can make a sigil, see pages 114–115, or perform a road-opening ritual (see page 91).

The challenge:

Take yourself on a walk – this can be anything from 10 minutes to an hour. Take a notepad and pen with you and, as you are moving, think about any stagnant energy in your body, specifically about what is holding you back or frustrating you. When you find a place to stop (this could be a park bench or a café – anywhere that isn't home) write down these thoughts. As you are walking home, slowly start to rip the piece of paper up, feeling lighter as you do. When the paper is fully ripped, find a receptacle to dispose of it, and know that when you walk through your front door, you have released it.

WEDNESDAY

Mercury, the planet of communication, brings about inciteful gifts and new ideas. Make the most of this planetary energy with a free-writing ritual. This is a great thing to do at sunrise, so consider getting up an hour earlier than you usually do.

YOU WILL NEED:

- *a pinch of frankincense*
- *a pinch of lavender*
- *a pinch of thyme*
- *a pen and paper*
- *a mortar and pestle*

The challenge:

In a clockwise direction, blend the herbs with a mortar and pestle. Follow the hot charcoal instructions on page 20. As the smoke travels, inhale and call for help from your spirit guides. Close your eyes, put pen to paper, and write. Allow the magical aroma of the smoke to guide your hand – don't even think about what you

are writing, just let the words pour from your heart. As you are writing, remind yourself that no-one will ever see this – the aim is to lose as much self-consciousness as possible, to get in touch with your inner self, and to understand your thoughts and feelings. Even you don't have to read it back if you don't want to; the importance is to get it out there. You can either dispose of the paper, or keep it somewhere safe.

THURSDAY

Jupiter brings with it abundance; this is a day to manifest!

The challenge:
Make an attraction oil – this will set you up for every Thursday to come.

YOU WILL NEED:

- *2 cinnamon sticks*
- *yellow string*
- *a magnet or lodestone crystal*
- *a Mason jar*
- *10 drops of patchouli essential oil*
- *9 cloves*
- *a pinch of dried basil*
- *20 ml (1 fl oz) of a carrier oil of your choice (I use sweet almond oil for everything, but any oil is fine)*

First, tie the cinnamon sticks together with the yellow string. Each time the string crosses over, repeat 'the Universe is always serving me for the best possible outcome'.

Put the cinnamon sticks and magnet in the jar with the rest of the ingredients. This is your attraction oil.

Take the pen and paper and write out your manifestations; see page 111 for guidance, if you need it.

Once written, take the cinnamon sticks out of the oil and anoint your piece of paper in a clockwise direction. Put the sticks back in the jar and fold the piece of paper towards you, turning clockwise with each fold. Keep it somewhere safe.

Note: at the next full moon, leave your oil jar outside in the moonlight to give it super-power.

FRIDAY

Friday is all about love; self-love and friendship. Use this day to express your gratitude and get in touch with your emotions.

The challenge:
Write a letter to a friend or family member you love. Let them know how grateful you are that they are in your life. Thank them for anything you feel they have helped you through, then either call them and tell them that you have something to read to them, or, even better, try the old fashioned way –

pop it in an envelope and post it to them.
Or be modern, and send an email.

SATURDAY

Saturn's day: time to get in touch with
yourself spiritually, release the stress
of your working week, and welcome
calm into your weekend.

The challenge:
Repeat a simple mantra as you meditate.
My top tip for when you are doing this
is not to set an alarm, but, instead start
a timer and come out of it naturally, as
opposed to having a beep or bell ringing.
Sit down comfortably, take a few long and
gentle breaths through your nose, close
your eyes and repeat the mantra 'I am
peace'. Do so for roughly 10 minutes.
It will only be natural for your mind to
welcome in other thoughts at this time –
that's ok, just remind yourself to go back
to the mantra when this happens.

'BE THANKFUL
FOR WHAT YOU
HAVE; YOU'LL
END UP HAVING
MORE. IF YOU
CONCENTRATE
ON WHAT YOU
DON'T HAVE,
YOU WILL NEVER,
EVER HAVE
ENOUGH.'

– OPRAH WINFREY

DAILY GRATITUDE CHALLENGE

Gratitude is a super-power that you have the skill to access at any time. You can create an internal magic within the brain; a magic that is so powerful that it can shift your mood in an instant, banish negative energy and raise your vibration, fast!

This super-power is always within you, ready and waiting to be summoned. There is no need for tools such as incense or crystals (although, obviously, anything you want to use to help you tap into it is always welcome).

Just remember that you don't have to think big. You can start with as little as thanking your lungs for your breath, or your eyes for being able to read this book, your hands for holding it, the money that was used to buy this book (or, perhaps, thankful for the friend who bought it for you!).

I feel that I must add a little bit of real talk here and acknowledge that gratitude is something that is a practice and that there is a possibility that you have just read this intro and may be feeling a little disconnected because you are feeling unable to connect to this energy. I want you to know that this is ok and that sometimes when the chips are down and life's challenges are hitting you hard, it is just not that easy to snap your fingers and feel happy or grateful about anything. If you are nodding your head right now and feeling this then please turn to pages 114–115 for a sigil spell.

Showing gratitude is a powerful way to show the Universe that you love yourself, but, that being said, you are totally allowed to feel all the feels. Happy, sad, emotional, excited, angry… all of them. It means you are a properly functioning human being with emotions and I'm pretty sure the Universe loves you being your authentic self even more.

Gratitude is a practice and the more practised you become, the easier it is to connect to this magical energy within the brain that can assist with uplifting your spirit and helping you to stay calm and balanced. This helps with your anxiety and trains you to control extreme reactions, to recover from life's knocks more easily, to banish fear and anger, and to celebrate life.

SIMPLE WAYS TO SHOW GRATITUDE

- Thank a tree for reminding you of the power and importance of nature.
- Send a message to a friend to let them know you are grateful for their presence in your life.
- When you are cooking, thank the ingredients for providing energy to fuel your life.
- Thank your heart for its openness and resilience.

DIVINATION

READING FORTUNES

There are many methods of reading fortunes, many with long histories; it can be seen as a form of guidance, to help make decisions, and to check in with your own intuition. The answers should be used to motivate, confirm your path, or point you in the right direction.

You may find that different methods work better than others when it comes to divination; it will depend on the areas that show up as being in need of assistance, from love-life to work goals. Interpreting information, tuning into your divine wisdom is one of the most powerful tools you can have; being able to look to yourself for guidance and bringing awareness to situations that need to be looked at is a very freeing skill.

Whether your feelings are based on fear or facts, just remember it takes practice to work out the difference.

It is important to remember that a reading will not always give you a definitive answer, you may not understand what you are told at that particular time, or you may wake up in the middle of the night and have a total 'aha!' moment. In the case of cartomancy (pages 158–168), you should make notes of what cards come up so that you can look back at a later date, to see what came true.

There are a few simple rules to follow across palmisty, cartomancy and tasseography, which are based mainly around cosmic ethics. Remember, never make decisions for anyone when you are giving them a reading, and don't share what you have read with anyone other than the person you have done the reading for. Remember that nothing is set in stone, if the reading tells you something you don't like the sound of, you have the power to change the outcome – take what was seen as a wake-up call or warning. Finally, at the end of a reading, always clap your hands three times to let the spiritual world know that you have closed the door on this reading.

Every type of fortune reading in this divination chapter could fill its own book (or books!). Use this as a guide to trying them to see which form of fortune-telling works for you.

PALMISTRY

Also known as chirology, palmistry
is an ancient art that is surrounded
by myth and intrigue. Studying the
details of a person's hands can reveal
characteristics and what the future
may hold.

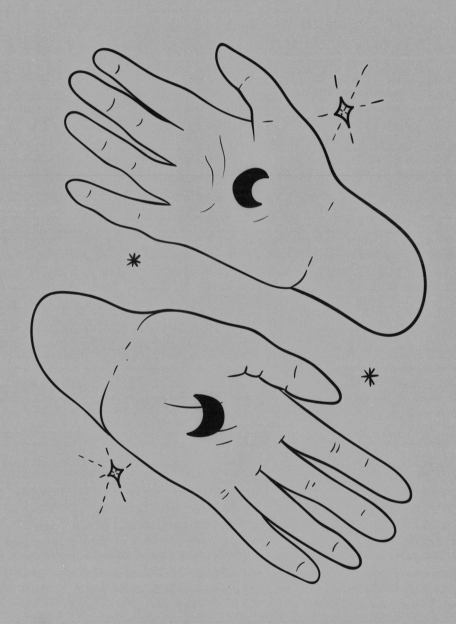

INTRODUCTION

When I was a kid, people would ask my mum if I played the piano, or would tell me if I didn't, that I should try, because I would be very good at it with my long fingers. At its heart, this example is the very basics of palm reading, and this is an observational skill that's universal.

As above, there are ways that you can instantly tell things about a person – a red palm signifying frustration, long fingers highlighting creativity, for example – but you will find more detailed descriptions of how to read palms on the following pages. I feel the below quote sums it up perfectly:

'If you look deeply into the palm of your hand, you will see your parents and all generations of your ancestors. All of them are alive in this moment; each is present in your body, and you are the continuation of these people.' (Thich Nhat Hanh)

HOW TO READ A PALM

The best way to start palm reading is to practise on yourself...

You will need a magnifying glass so you can see your palm lines close-up.

Start with reading the dominant hand. The dominant hand represents what has gone on, what is going on and what is going to happen in the future.

Always start a palm reading by taking the

palm you are reading in your hands and hold it for a little while. Take some time to notice if your intuition is giving you messages, notice if you are feeling anything – this may be in the form of a vision, words that are popping up in your head or an energy shift in your body.

Each feature of the hand can be interpreted.

FLEXIBILITY

Notice how flexible the hand is, do the fingers bend back and away from the palm? This movement shows how flexible and easy going a person is.

- If it **bends back with ease**, you are a very easy going person.

- If it **doesn't move back** this indicates stubbornness.

THUMBS

Do the thumbs bend back? The further they bend, the more generous someone is.

COLOUR OF THE PALM

- A **pink** palm signifies happiness and contentedness. This shows the person has good vibes and a positive and peaceful outlook on life.

- A **red** palm can mean that the person is frustrated and has some stuff that

they need to get off their chest. It can mean that they can easily lose their temper and are very sensitive.

- A **white** palm indicates that person is a little low on energy, maybe weighed down by confusion and not trusting their inner voice.

- A **yellow** palm can represent anxiety; a person with a yellow hand may be unable to speak up and tell their truth.

FINGERS

- If the **ring finger is longer than the index finger**, this is a sign of confidence, but this person may be unbalanced.

- If the **index finger is longer than the ring finger** this shows creativity, but this person might find it hard to make decisions.

- If the **index finger is the same length as the ring finger** this shows that this person is well balanced and decisive.

- **Long fingers** signify creativity and good attention to detail. Long fingered people are usually thoughtful and quite sensitive, but can also be disorganised.

- **Short fingered** people can lack patience, they like to take care of business and get stuff ticked off their to do list. They are good at reaching goals and are usually very successful with their career.

PALM SHAPES

FIRE

A fire hand has a long palm and short fingers; a hand like this will show that the person is full of energy and very enthusiastic about life. Sometimes they may lack empathy and not have a full emotional understanding of other people's troubles.

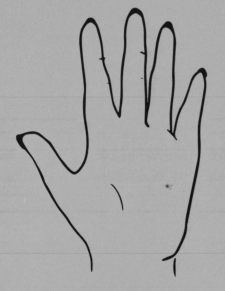

WATER

Water hands have a long palm and long fingers; those who have them are usually very creative, with a good imagination. A sensitive soul, who feels deep empathy and compassion. Those with water hands are good at connecting to their intuition and are often attracted to the metaphysical world and the unseen.

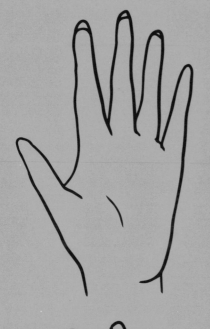

AIR

An air hand has a square-shaped palm and long fingers; air hands are practical thinkers, they are good at coming up with ideas and problem solving. Those with these hands are gentle souls and are loyal friends.

EARTH

Earth hands have a square-shaped palm and short fingers; people with earth hands are very grounded and down to earth. They like to have stability and security around them and are usually very family orientated.

FOUR MAJOR

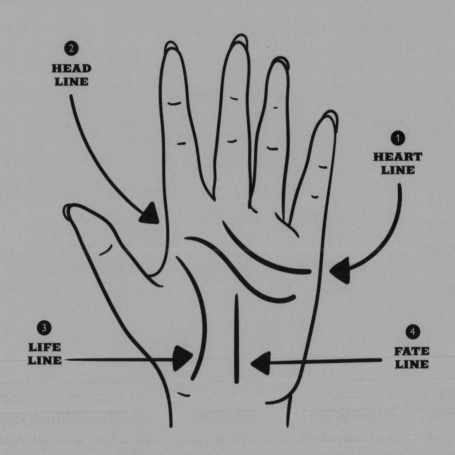

2 HEAD LINE

1 HEART LINE

3 LIFE LINE

4 FATE LINE

PALM LINES

THE HEART LINE

The heart line is all about love and emotions. A heart line will often show up relationships and how someone behaves in relationships.

- If this line goes **up in the direction of your fingers** it can represent a jealous nature in matters of the heart.

- If it goes **straight across** this can mean you are not in touch with your emotions.

- If it goes **up towards the middle finger**, it can show heartache.

- If it **begins far below the middle finger** it indicates selfishness in love.

- If it **begins beneath the middle finger**, then you fall easily in love.

- A **big curve** in the heart line symbolises that you find it easy to express your emotions.

THE HEAD LINE

The head line shows the way someone thinks and what motivates them.

- A **straight** head line represents a logical thinker.

- A **zig-zag** line shows that the mind may wander and find it difficult to focus.

- If this line **curves downwards** it shows an easily trusting person.

- If it is **curved upwards** it shows the person to be spontanious and creative.

- Those with a **wavy** head line will have a short attention span and like to move around.

- If the head line is **deep set** it indicates a very focused mind, and probably someone quite academic.

THE LIFE LINE

This line does not have anything to do with how long your life will be! It shows what direction your life, experiences and energy will go in.

- If this line is **deep**, it indicates you are strong minded and focussed on achieving goals.

- If this line is **faint** you may be easily distracted.

- A **zig-zag** life line shows you like to try many things in life and always have lots of projects on the go.

- If there is a **break in the life line**, it might indicate a sudden change, like moving to a different country or a career change.

- If it's **curvy** you probably have lots of energy and are a fun person to be around.

THE FATE LINE

This is the line that shows your destiny and which way everything in your life is heading; think decisions about support, life goals and love.

- If this line is **short,** it means that you are a chilled out person; advice would be to focus your energy on something that inspires you to give you a firmer footing in life.

- If this line is **long,** it means there is great success to come. It may also indicate being a workaholic.

- Any **changes or crosses** going over the fate line will predict great life changes, inevitably for the better. Many forks mean that you will have many choices.

FINGERTIPS

Each person has only one type of fingerprint, and thus corresponding life path. Start by looking on your index finger, as this will be the clearest, and represents what you feel about yourself. The old-fashioned way of doing this is with a microscope, but you can easily take a zoomed in picture on your phone to inspect more closely.

THE WAVE
LIFE PATH:
Responsibility

THE COMET
LIFE PATH:
The heart

THE TENT
LIFE PATH:
Courage

THE WHIRLPOOL
LIFE PATH:
The teacher

'LIFE WILL
GIVE YOU
WHATEVER
EXPERIENCE IS
THE MOST
HELPFUL
FOR YOUR
EVOLUTION OF
CONSCIOUSNESS.'

– ECKHART TOLLE

THE SOLAR SYSTEM

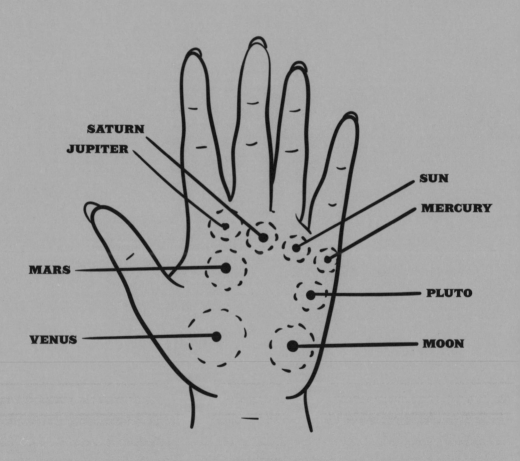

ON PALMS

THE SOLAR SYSTEM ON PALMS

Each planet stands for different characteristics. Looking at the mounds can indicate lifestyle choices, career moves or love.

Jupiter

This represents career, will-power and ambition. If the bump is high, then you are likely to be driven in all endeavours, and your work-life will be prominent. If it's low, this means your work isn't the centre of your existence.

Saturn

This indicates the way you look at life. If this is high, it means you are likely to be emotional and less of a risk taker. If it is low, you might be a bit of a loner, and very in touch with the spiritual world.

Sun

This shows special interests and your outlook on life. If it is high, you have many interests and are good at retaining information. A lower bump indicates that your interests lie in the factual – think documentaries over films.

Mercury

This represents your inner wisdom. If you have a decent-sized bump, you are resourceful and don't have any difficulty in making friends with strangers. A lower mound may indicate that you are a little bit of an introvert and enjoy your own company.

Pluto

This represents rebirth. A larger bump may indicate a big life change, leading to a new path in midlife. If you don't have much definition, it might mean that life events are relatively stable.

Moon

This is related to intuition and the unseen. If this is big, then you are likely to be a very intuitive person and have a great imagination. If it's low, you perhaps prefer more structure and routine in your life.

Venus

This is the symbol of love and relationships. If you have a larger mound, you are more likely to have a big sexual appetite, fall in love easily and feel deep empathy with others. If you have a smaller mound, use it as a reminder to nurture yourself. It also shows that you might be attracted to a partner's personality rather than their looks.

Mars

This is the area of thoughts and decision-making. If you have a big bump, this shows that you put your well-being first, and that you are good at taking care of yourself. If it is smaller, you don't have very much self control, and are less adventurous.

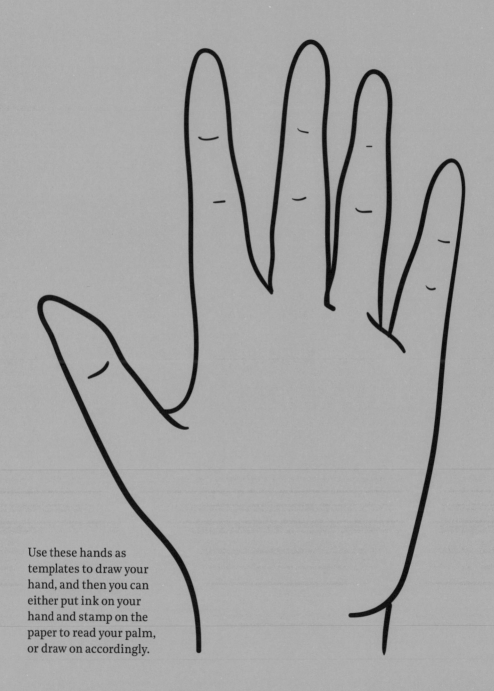

Use these hands as
templates to draw your
hand, and then you can
either put ink on your
hand and stamp on the
paper to read your palm,
or draw on accordingly.

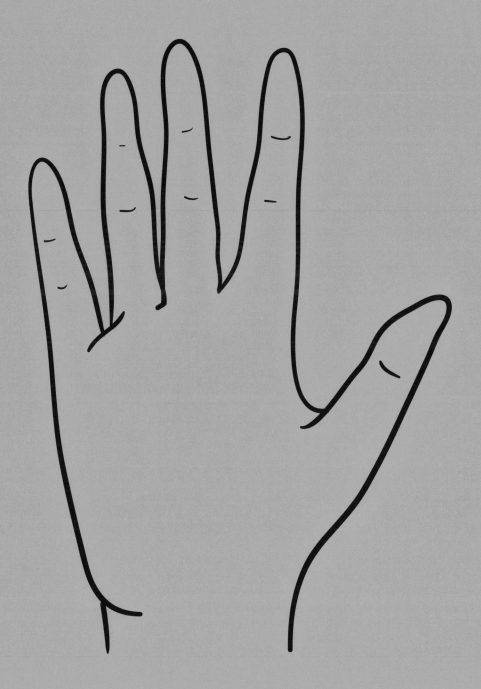

CARTOMANCY

Connect with the cards, allow their power to shine a spotlight on what you already know and confirm questions your intuition is asking.

INTRODUCTION

Fortune telling with cards is all about reading the symbolic associations of the suits and numbers in the deck. Also, the numbers can represent dates and times that are significant to you. So, for example, you could ask for a specific date for when something might happen, or you could add these numbers up and research what the numerology reading of the resulting number would be.

This is a great tool with which to start exercising your intuition. Begin by doing a three-card reading, with a very specific question in mind – this can be anything from 'Will I have a change in my life soon?' to 'Am I focussing my energy in the right direction?'.

It's important to practise on yourself first, just to get a feel for the method. You can ask a whole array of questions to get a better understanding of how the answers come through and how to interpret them. When you feel ready, you can begin to give readings to friends, either one-on-one or in a group. There's no reason not to make a night of it. As you use the cards, you may connect with some of them in your own way, differing with the meaning that you will find in the following pages. Keep a record of your own meanings to check against future readings.

Face cards (Jack, Queen or King) –
may represent qualities and traits in
your personality that you have or that you
need to draw upon, or they may signify
people who are already in your life or
who are about to come into your life.

Numbers – give advice on life events
that are coming.

Diamonds – represent material items,
financial matters and work-life.

Hearts – represent love, relationships,
your feelings and emotions.

Spades – represent challenges you
may face and solutions to get you to
the next level.

Clubs – highlight what you should focus
on, what needs to be brought to attention.

PAST, PRESENT, FUTURE –
HOW TO LAY OUT YOUR CARDS

*You can do a three-card reading
or just pick one card.*

Hold the cards in your less dominant
hand and with the other hand, knock
on the deck three times, then shuffle.
As you shuffle think of a question.

THREE-CARD SPREAD

If you are doing a three-card spread, pull out three cards and lay them down left to right. The cards should be read from left to right.

These cards all signify questions you may be asking about:

- Your past, your present or your future

- Your situation, an obstacle or a solution

- What you think, what you feel or what you do

- Your strengths and weaknesses, and advice you need

- You, your partner or your relationship – What do you want? What do they want? Where is the relationship heading?

Or if you are feeling indecisive, give yourself three options and have each card represent each option.

READING
THE
PLAYING
CARDS

DIAMONDS

A♦ *Ace of Diamonds*
Good news is coming: a new beginning. You are entering a new phase of your life.

2♦ *Two of Diamonds*
Financial partnerships are paying off, small payments are being received (financial and energetic).

3♦ *Three of Diamonds*
You are clearing debt or other obstacles. Remember to be true to yourself and keep your eyes on the prize.

4♦ *Four of Diamonds*
Be open to advice and welcome help from those around you.

5♦ *Five of Diamonds*
Successful meetings and supportive relationships surround you.

6♦ *Six of Diamonds*
This is a good time to network – get yourself out there.

7♦ *Seven of Diamonds*
A surprise is coming, you will gain rewards and recognition for your efforts.

8♦ *Eight of Diamonds*
You are about to face a big, life-changing decision.

9♦ *Nine of Diamonds*
Trust that everything is moving at the right pace and everything will be happening at the right time.

10♦ *Ten of Diamonds*
Big money is on its way to you.

J♦ *Jack of Diamonds*
A dynamic younger person (male or female) has good ideas that might be able to assist with your manifestations.

Q♦ *Queen of Diamonds*
This woman is a powerhouse. She is very well connected, gives great advice regarding business and is here to remind you to treat yourself, have fun and enjoy the finer things in life.

K♦ *King of Diamonds*
This guy is a success – he may be an entrepreneur. He is confident and ambitious! A loyal friend, someone you can depend on, a mentor, well respected.

HEARTS

A♥ *Ace of Hearts*
True love and happiness.
Romance is coming and deep
connections are shared.

2♥ *Two of Hearts*
You are supported and have great
friends around you. A love affair
may be coming.

3♥ *Three of Hearts*
Change is coming. Emotions
that have been running high
will be coming to an end.

4♥ *Four of Hearts*
Positive outcomes are on their way.

5♥ *Five of Hearts*
Watch your back – someone may be
jealous of you. Keep your friends
close and your enemies closer.

6♥ *Six of Hearts*
Nurture yourself and those you
love. Feel lucky and you will
be lucky.

7♥ *Seven of Hearts*
A decision must be made –
personal growth is strong.

8♥ *Eight of Hearts*
Reuniting with old friends and
lovers. Slow down so you can take
in all that is happening and feel
balanced and calm.

9♥ *Nine of Hearts*
Make a wish and your dreams will
come true. Positive outcomes are
on the way.

10♥ *Ten of Hearts*
Spiritual and material abundance
are on their way to you.

J♥ *Jack of Hearts*
A young man with a lightness of
heart looking for a relationship,
however fleeting it may be.

Q♥ *Queen of Hearts*
A compassionate woman – maybe
a healer – that you can trust and
receive good nurturing advice from.

K♥ *King of Hearts*
Helpful and kind – good advice
is there for the taking.

SPADES

A♠ *Ace of Spades*
Death. The same as in the tarot,
a death means a new beginning.
One door closes and another opens.

2♠ *Two of Spades*
A tricky situation could be ahead.
Be ready for conflict.

3♠ *Three of Spades*
Miscommunication. Review
your actions.

4♠ *Four of Spades*
Rest and relax, take a back seat
and take care of yourself.

5♠ *Five of Spades*
Obstacles and hold-ups may be
blessings in disguise. Lie low
and be patient.

6♠ *Six of Spades*
Completion and satisfaction. Now
is the time for a transformation.

7♠ *Seven of Spades*
Beware of disagreements –
check your motives.

8♠ *Eight of Spades*
Take action. Break free from
anything holding you back.

9♠ *Nine of Spades*
Call in your courage and
determination right now. Tune
into your intuition for guidance.

10♠ *Ten of Spades*
Emotional pain you have endured
is holding you back. It is important
to heal these wounds.

J♠ *Jack of Spades*
A young person who may be
travelling or unsettled in life.
Inconsistent in their emotions and
values, they may take from
you and drain your energy.

Q♠ *Queen of Spades*
A woman who speaks the truth,
she may sometimes sound harsh but
you can trust her and confide in her.

K♠ *King of Spades*
A trustworthy man who is strong
willed and good natured. He
appears to remain calm at all times
and can step in as a good mediator.
Sometimes he may appear
emotionally unavailable.

CLUBS

A♣ Ace of Clubs
Learn new things, as you will
be adding strings to your bow.

2♣ Two of Clubs
There may be obstacles in your way
right now. Communication is key;
look for signs.

3♣ Three of Clubs
Trust the creative process and know
that your efforts have been noticed.

4♣ Four of Clubs
Take care of yourself, slow down,
and recharge. Expect calm after
the storm.

5♣ Five of Clubs
Confusion – you may need to call
in the help of friends to help you
see things clearly.

6♣ Six of Clubs
Your intuition is strong.
Trust your gut feelings.

7♣ Seven of Clubs
Speak up, don't be shy and stick
up for what you believe in, but
remember – delivery is everything.

8♣ Eight of Clubs
Miscommunication may cause
problems in the workplace.

9♣ Nine of Clubs
Completion is near – your
determination will pay off. You
may have difficulty in letting go
of something but try to move on.

10♣ Ten of Clubs
A lot of hard work lies ahead.
Try not to take too many risks.

J♣ Jack of Clubs
A friend who you can count on.
Practical and helpful when help
is needed in stressful situations.

Q♣ Queen of Clubs
She has good ideas and her approval
can help validate any projects or
ideas you may be involved in.

K♣ King of Clubs
Master of communication,
with a deep wisdom to assist
in bringing success.

'FOLLOW YOUR INSTINCTS. THAT IS WHERE TRUE WISDOM MANIFESTS ITSELF.'

– OPRAH WINFREY

TASSEOGRAPHY

The history of tea leaf reading, or tasseography, is long and varied. While it originated in ancient China, possibly thousands of years ago, its popularity in Europe spread in the Victorian period as a result of nomadic communities and a general fascination with the occult.

INTRODUCTION

Part of the reason that fortune-telling has always felt so familiar to me is that my grandmother was a very gifted Turkish coffee-cup reader. I remember everyone gathering around, drinking coffee, transfixed by the fortunes that she could see in their cups. Her readings were infamous in the Turkish community of North London, and, as a result, my interest in magic began at an early age.

Tea-leaf reading, or tasseography, is more widely accessible and well known, but, as with everything in this book, you must do what feels the most natural to you. So, if you have Turkish coffee to hand, then feel free to experiment and do some more research in this area. Turkish coffee reading uses similar symbols, so you can use tasseography readings as a rough guide.

But, anyway, back to the tea. When it comes to reading for others, the reading can start at the point of pouring into the cup. As you ask the person to think of their question as they are drinking their tea, you can use this time to awaken your intuition and see if you are picking up anything from their energy. For tips on intuition, see page 184.

In all of these instances, as the reader, it is important that you feel calm and open to receiving messages. As the person being read, you should be relaxed and open-minded, ready to take notes of any of the signs and symbols that have presented themselves, as they have a funny way of showing their relevance in the days and weeks to come. Lastly, when it comes to saying what you have intuited, don't be afraid of getting something wrong. If you feel that you've been given a message, it's always worth passing it on. Interpretation can of course take many forms, and, once again, it's about practise.

SETTING UP YOUR READING

> **YOU WILL NEED:**
>
> - *1 teaspoon of loose black tea leaves*
> - *a light-coloured tea cup and saucer*

01 Place the tea leaves in your cup and add boiling water to fill the cup. Give the tea a little stir.

02 As the hot water starts to cool and the tea leaves sink to the bottom of the cup, start sipping on your tea and thinking of a question that you would like the tea leaves to answer. Focus on this question as you drink your tea.

03 Drink all of the tea, leaving about a teaspoon of liquid in the tea cup. Place the saucer over the top of the tea cup and ask your question. Then turn the cup three times in a clockwise direction.

04 Leave your cup upside down on the saucer for a minute or so (or until the time feels right) and allow any of the remaining liquid to drain out on to the saucer.

05 Turn your cup the right way up and begin to look for messages in the tea cup. Start by looking for any concentrated formations or clusters of leaves, these indicate a timeline (see illustration overleaf).

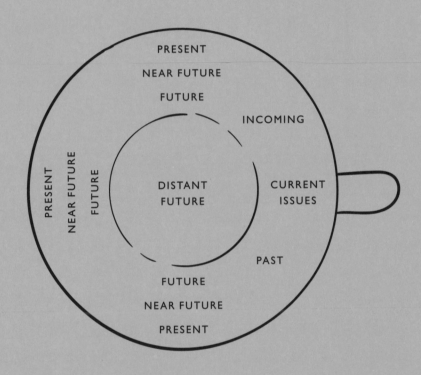

PAST, PRESENT, FUTURE

If the leaves are forming a message close to the handle of the tea cup, then what you are seeing will be happening directly to you. The formations around this part of the cup represent current issues and what is on your mind at this time.

Towards the right-hand side of the handle is what is incoming and towards the left-hand side of the handle is what you have moved on from and is now in the past.

Anything towards the rim of the cup will be happening very soon, probably within days. If these formations are around the middle section of the tea cup, within weeks, and, if there is a formation towards the bottom of the cup, this will represent events happening in the distant future.

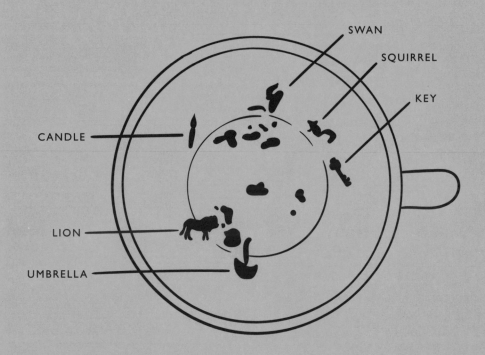

CANDLE

SWAN

SQUIRREL

KEY

LION

UMBRELLA

FINDING SHAPES

Move the cup around, look at it from different angles and always go with your first impressions of what the shapes are saying to you, as these first visions are usually very intuitive. Look for letters, animals, numbers, shapes and any feelings that any of the shapes give you.

Do you feel excited or scared? Always try and remember your initial feelings.

See overleaf for shape interpretations.

HOW TO INTERPRET SHAPES
YOU MAY SEE IN YOUR TEA CUP

Use this as a rough guide to signs
and symbols that you might see in
a cup, but I strongly advise that you
use your intuition; a lion might mean
that you need to find courage, or,
it could relate to a Leo in your life.
Look out for numbers, letters or any
other symbols that might be personal
to you or the person who is being
read for in addition to those listed.
Pay special attention to how you feel,
as they are trying to speak to you and
carry a message. Finally, be patient
with yourself – the art of reading
takes practise.

Aeroplane	you will travel
Angel	good news is coming
Axe	hex is broken, your troubles are over
Birds	good luck, good news is coming your way
Boat	you will hear from a friend who is far away
Butterfly	success is coming
Candle	embrace your spiritual side
Car	you are approaching an important stage of your life
Castle	money is coming
Chain	the start of a chain of events
Circles	a project or relationship is close to completion
Clover	it is OK to ask for help
Coffin	something is coming to an end, a new beginning is approaching
Cow	money is coming
Dog	a friend needs help
Door closed	you have missed opportunities
Door open	new opportunities will come to you
Ear	good news is coming
Egg	a good omen
Feather	lack of concentration
Fish	good news is coming
Flowers	you will find happiness in romance

Four leaf clover	good luck		**Padlock (open)**	a happy surprise is coming
Gun	there's trouble ahead		**Ring**	a commitment
Horse shoe	lucky partner		**Scissors**	a separation, breaking away
Hourglass	there's an important decision to be made		**Shoe**	happy changes
House	you will have success in business		**Snake**	a new beginning, a rebirth
			Spider	your hard work is paying off
Kettle	a death		**Spoon**	a generous gift is on its way
Key	major life improvements ahead		**Squirrel**	you need to save money
			Star	fame awaits
Keyhole	trust your inner voice		**Swan**	a happy love life
Kite	your wish will come true		**Teddy**	children
Knife	disagreements		**Trees**	you will have good luck, contentment
Ladder	your life is improving			
Lamp	success is coming		**Turtle**	slow progress
Lion	you have influential friends		**UFO**	your psychic ability should be explored
Lizard (any reptile)	watch your back			
			Umbrella	you are protected
Lobster	a big event is coming		**Vase**	a friend will need your help
Magnet	it's the perfect time to manifest what you want		**Volcano**	uncontrollable emotions
			Watch	act fast, stop procrastinating
Man	a man is coming into your life			
			Woman	a woman is coming into your life
Mask	insecurities			
Moon (crescent)	prosperity			
Moon (full)	happiness			
Mountain	overcoming fears and obstacles			
Padlock (closed)	protect yourself			

PAPER
ORACLES

'I used to be indecisive, but now
I'm not so sure.' This always makes
me laugh and if, like me, you have
moments of being totally indecisive,
or just need a tool for a little daily
guidance, then a paper oracle is the
perfect tool to assist your decisions.
See overleaf for instructions on how
to make one.

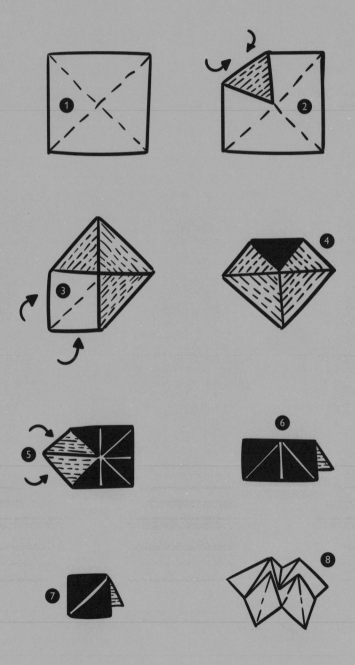

PAPER ORACLE INSTRUCTIONS

01 Take a square of paper – this can be any size you like, mine is 22 x 22 cm (8.7 x 8.7 in). Fold the paper in half diagonally to make a triangle. Fold in half again to make a smaller triangle, then unfold to reveal the 'X' crease across the paper.

02 Fold the top left-hand corner of the paper into the centre, to the middle of the 'X'.

03 Repeat with the other three corners. You should end up with a smaller square.

04 Flip the square over and repeat the process.

05 You should end up with an even smaller square.

06 Horizontally fold the bottom edge of the square up to the top of the square, then unfold.

07 Fold the left-hand side of the square vertically in half to meet the right-hand side of the square, then unfold. You will now have a star pattern of creases on your square.

08 Next, push your fingertips into the flaps of the four corners of the square, and then bring them together. Your paper oracle should now move like a puppet with your fingers.

At this point, following the suggestions below or making your own, you can personalise your oracle. As a rule of thumb, write four symbols (I use a pentagram, an eye, a crystal and a wand) on the outside flaps, the numbers one to eight on the eight triangles on the reverse side of this, then unfold and write eight fortunes in the middle.

RITUAL ORACLE
Fortunes: do a moon ritual, do the sunrise ritual, pick a daily ritual, make a sigil, do a chakra ritual, do an astrological moon ritual, do a smoke cleansing ritual, do the full daily ritual challenge

DAILY MANTRA ORACLE
Fortunes: I am love, I am open to change, I am consciousness, I am raising my vibration, I am nature, I am free to be myself, I am peace

COLOUR ORACLE
Fortunes: wear red to release your inner power, wear blue to be at peace, wear yellow to open the road, wear pink to express compassion, wear white to shine your light, wear green to welcome in abundance, wear purple to open your intuition, wear orange to express courage

QUOTE ORACLE
Fortunes: Oprah quote, Eckhart Tolle quote, Rob Breszny quote, Ram Dass quote, Dalai Lama quote, Deepak Chopra quote, Rhonda Byrne quote, Louise Hay quote

SIGNS FROM THE UNIVERSE

When you look around and tune in, you will notice that the Universe is constantly providing you with signs and signals. Learning how to read them and what these messages mean can be helpful ways to know you are on the right path, and to remind you that everything is connected.

INTUITION

This, in essence, is all about chatting with your inner voice. Everyone knows that feeling – a turn in your stomach when you shouldn't go somewhere, or even date someone – but you do it anyway. You've probably kicked yourself for it afterwards, too. This is about learning how to tune in and trust that voice. It takes practise to work out the difference between fear and fact with intuition; it's always asking yourself the question, however sure you think you are initially.

Tuning into your intuition isn't only listening to your inner voice – it's about receiving answers and signs from your ancestors and spirit guides, as well as signs from the Universe. The more you can develop and trust your intuition, the less frequent moments of doubt, frustration of confusion will arise. As I said, this is very much practise-based, and often a test of patience. If your head is busy and your body is stressed, it's likely that you will be receiving answers from a place of panic or fear, as opposed to your higher self.

WAYS TO COMMUNICATE WITH YOUR INTUITION

- Ask the question, and notice any feelings in your body; if you notice an energy in any particular part of your body, consider why that might be. For extra guidance, see pages 54–67 for information about chakras.

- You may have had a vision in a dream, or had something pop into your head when you were meditating – don't ignore it, take time to explore it!

- Learn to recognise how your inner voice communicates with you – this may be having the confidence to label a moment of clarity as your intuition, or taking a glimmer of sudden inspiration as the beginning of a chat with your intuition.

Intuition applies across the board in cosmic communication – remind yourself of this page when you are calling things in, reading fortunes and even creating daily rituals. The first voice will eventually become the loudest.

'THE TRUE
SOLVER OF
PROBLEMS IS
INTUITION.'

– DEEPAK CHOPRA

SYNCHRONICITIES

Synchronicities are the Universe's way of communicating with us. These are cosmic gifts presented to us by our spirit guides to help us along the way, to teach us, inspire us, reassure us and remind us that there is an otherness connecting us at all times.

You may have overheard a conversation on a bus that was relevant to what you were thinking at the time, bumped into an old friend or work colleague who you were meant to reconnect with, received a phone call from someone just as you were thinking about them or found yourself opening a book or a magazine to see a caption that applied to the particular thought that you were having at that exact moment.

All of these signs are here to remind you that there is more going on at an energetic level than meets the eye, and taking note of these synchronicities is to acknowledge your higher self. You will probably find that once you start connecting to the signs you will start to see them all the time, and the more you tune in, the more you will be able to use them as valuable tools to guide you.

Another common way for the Universe to connect with us is by showing us repeating numbers. You may look at the time and it's 11.11 or see the same sets of repeating numbers in receipts, registration plates, telephone numbers, door numbers or a particular number that means something to you.

These numbers may be showing up to remind you that you are an energetic, magical force of nature, and to reassure you that you are exactly where you need to be at this precise moment.

When you keep seeing the same set of numbers, there is a chance that they may be trying to communicate a more specific message. Try to take notice – what was on your mind at the exact moment you've saw these numbers?

If you have been seeing:

1111

MEGA POSITIVE! These magical numbers are here to let you know that everything is aligned perfectly and you are exactly where you need to be right now. You are moving in the right direction.

Be conscious of your thoughts and actions when you are tuned into the alignment of 1111, as the energy that you are putting out into the Universe at this time will be the energy that is coming back to you. Take a moment to perform a random act of kindness, and remind yourself of something you are grateful for.

AFFIRMATION: *I am grateful for all of the amazing things in my life and I give them power to grow and multiply.*

2222

The number 2 in numerology represents relationships, so this could mean you should take time to focus on your connection with yourself or with someone close to you.

If you see these numbers, take note – how is your inner voice communicating with you? Are you talking to yourself in a friendly way? These numbers may be reminding you to take better care of yourself on a spiritual level, a reminder to connect through a spiritual practice such as meditating or calling in on the power of crystals.

How are your relationships working out? Do you have anything to work out with a lover, friend or family member? Take this time to reconnect and let them know how you are feeling. Are you looking for love? If so, these numbers might be showing up to let you know a new lover might be on their way to you.

AFFIRMATION: *I am love and I move through life filled with peace and harmony.*

3333

You are tuning into the powers of 3333 as the Universe wants you to know that you are unconditionally loved and supported. Your spirit guides are all around you and they want to communicate that they have your back.

You may have a decision to make or a question to ask at this time. Feel free to ask them for more signs and guidance, and see what they present you with.

If you have recently made a big change in your life, these numbers are here to tell you that you made the correct decision.

AFFIRMATION: *I am protected and I am loved.*

4444

These numbers are here to let you know that the time has come for you to make an upgrade in your spiritual practices. You are ready for the next level!

You may find that you are feeling like you are awakening and connecting to a higher energy. If, around this time, you are feeling curious or wanting to learn something new, then this is your green light.

Your intuition is strong at this time, your psychic energy is ready to be put into action. This is a great time to take up tarot or palm reading. Wake your third eye up by tapping on it gently with your middle and index fingers. You have the knowledge within you to tell you what your next step should be.

AFFIRMATION: *I am connected to the Universe and I have nothing to fear.*

5555

Everything that you have been through and all of your life lessons have brought you to this point. A big change has either just happened or is about to happen and the 5s are here to let you know it

is time to move on. You are ready for a bit of a shake up. Don't be afraid to let go of the past – when one door closes and another opens.

This is a time of personal growth and new opportunities. Tap into this energy flow and set your intentions – visualise them, talk about them and write them down. Don't be afraid to take a risk. Trust in the Universe and go, go, go!!!

AFFIRMATION: *I will break free of my past and look forward to a brighter future.*

6666

This is a sign to give yourself a little TLC maybe you've been working harder than usual or are feeling stressed.

Allow these numbers to give you permission to treat yourself. Cook yourself something really special for dinner or get your favourite takeaway, go shopping, have a massage, take a nap.

Nurture yourself and don't feel guilty about it. Show the Universe that you know how to be kind to yourself.

AFFIRMATION: *I always take time for me.*

7777

Lucky, lucky, lucky! Gifts from the Universe are making their way to you – luck, money, love – they are all there for the taking. The Universe is rewarding you as an acknowledgement of the work you have been putting in. If you have currently started a spiritual practice, this is a sign that it is the right thing, so embrace it. You are tuned into your life purpose, you are powerful, you are magical.

This is a great time to make a sigil to represent your mood, so you can retain this abundant moment (see pages 114–115).

AFFIRMATION: *I am attracting miracles.*

8888

Change is coming. If you have been feeling a little stuck, experiencing blocks or feeling some of life's challenges, 8888 is here to let you know that it's not your fault and not to worry as change is coming.

Emotional breakthroughs, changes to your financial situation and shifts in energy are coming your way. Expect to feel a new sense of freedom. Success and personal power are on their way to you. Let these numbers encourage you to carry on and push forward just a little bit more – you are almost there.

AFFIRMATION: *I have the power to create all of the personal success I desire.*

9999

The number 9 in numerology represents completion, so, if you are seeing 9s, it is time to banish negative energy from the past. Burn some sage to shake up any

stagnant energy that is surrounding you, cut any emotional cords that are holding you back, clear out the clutter from your home. This is a time for closure and you are ready to move onwards and upwards.

You are at the end of a big learning phase in your life, which will have given you a better understanding of the world. You are about to turn into a butterfly. Abundance and wonderful things await you as your transformation takes place.

AFFIRMATION: *I welcome and embrace the powerful changes that are happening.*

0000

Just like a new moon or the beginning of a new season, seeing 0000 brings new beginnings. This is a perfect time to set intentions and goals for new projects and practices. This is such a good time to embrace acting on an idea that you have been putting off.

You are currently operating on a high-vibing frequency, so look out for signs from the Universe. You may be more in tune, noticing symbols and having psychic visions, or meeting people who could be helpful to you. Take note, as all of these things are in place to give you guidance, and to help you to move forward and proceed.

AFFIRMATION: *There are no limitations.*

OMENS

Omens are perhaps one the most well-documented forms of signs from the Universe. While, as with synchronicities, their purpose is to give guidance and support, omens can often snowball in their appearance once you are aware of their significance.

As with tasseography (pages 170–177) and palm reading (pages 144–157), the following examples of omens and their meanings are very much dependent on a co-existence with your own intuition. In these circumstances, it is important to listen to your inner voice first, and then use this guide to interpret.

BIRDS

If a bird poops on you this signifies that good fortune is coming your way – so make a wish before you clean it up!

CROWS

The significance of an encounter with crows depends on how many crows you see.

1   be extra vigilant
2   bring good luck
3   bring good health
4   bring wealth
5   bring sickness
6   bring death

MAGPIES

Magpies are gatekeepers of the other dimension – salute them to acknowledge the metaphysical world.

OWLS

Owls are omens of success. If you see an owl three days after casting a spell, this means that your magic is working.

SNAKES

Snakes signify rebirth, new beginnings and transformation.

SPIDERS

If a spider shows itself to you it is telling you to be patient, your wishes are on their way to you.

To see your initials in a spider's web signifies good luck forever!

CATS

White cats are a sign of fertility or that change is coming in your love life.

If a black cat walks towards you it's a sign of good luck, and if it walks away from you it takes its luck with it.

LADYBIRDS

Ladybirds (ladybugs) are messengers of joy.

BUTTERFLIES

Butterflies are messengers from the other side, reminding you to think of a loved one who is watching over you.

EYES TWITCHING

If your right eye twitches, expect to hear of a birth. If your left eye twitches, expect to hear of a death.

A FALLEN EYELASH

Place the eyelash on the back of your hand, blow it and make a wish. If it flies away your wish will be granted.

ITCHY FEET

If you have itchy feet this signifies you will travel.

ITCHY EARS

If you have an itchy ear this means someone is talking about you. If it's your left ear, they are saying nice things and, if they are saying something nasty your right ear will itch (right for spite, left for love). If you say the name of the person who you think is talking about you out loud and get it right, the itching will stop.

ITCHY HANDS

If your left palm itches or tingles this signifies money is coming in and if your right palm itches and tingles money is going out.

IF YOU FIND A COIN

If you find a coin, it's good luck to pick it up if it's tail-side up, and bad luck to pick it up if it's head-side up.

'BEING
AT EASE
WITH NOT
KNOWING IS
CRUCIAL FOR
ANSWERS TO
COME
TO YOU.'

– ECKHART TOLLE

CEREMONIES

SPIRITUAL CEREMONIES

Ceremonies can act as important markers, whether that's to celebrate the changing of the seasons, or to get together with friends to honour your relationships.

INTRODUCTION

Whether in a group or alone, harnessing the empowering, positive energies that surround us, especially at times such as solstices and equinoxes, can go a long way to making us feel energised, grounded, and full of cosmic joy.

Among friends, spiritual ceremonies are a beautiful way of uniting together, setting positive intentions and celebrating your connections. Take it from me, there is nothing like sharing the summer solstice sunrise with a few very special friends (and crystals like Charmaine, see page 96 to hear more about her).

If the changing seasons present themselves as moments for quiet reflection, a ceremony is a wonderful way to dedicate some time to yourself, and yourself alone. Equally, if you are feeling slightly disconnected, or need to recentre your energies, then tuning into Mother Nature is a sure-fire way of slipping back into synch with the Universe.

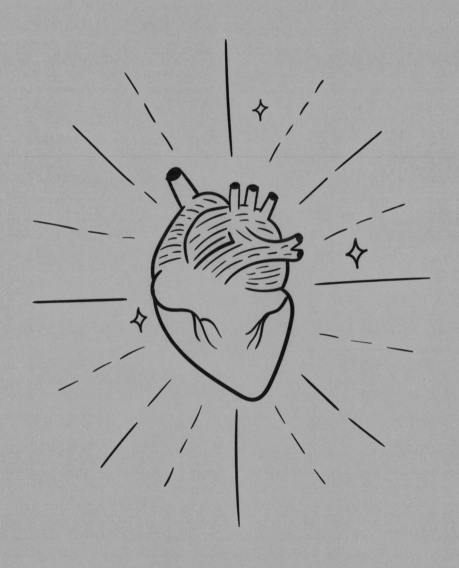

FRIENDSHIP CIRCLE GROUP TEA CEREMONY

Gathering with friends and creating a ceremony is a powerful way to connect and affirm friendships. Taking time to share stories, and show each other love and support.

INSTRUCTIONS FOR A TEA CEREMONY

The host should send invites out two weeks prior to the ceremony. An electronic invite is OK here, but I think that an invite by post makes the event much more magical.

The invite should include what the shared intention will be; in this case a heart-opening ritual, but any joint intention can work here. (Remember, when you join forces and set an intention together the magic and energy will be super-charged.)

On the invites ask your guests to think about what they might like to share. It may be a positive story, an uplifting life lesson they have learnt, something they have researched about the current astrological energy, tarot cards, a craft project that everyone can participate in, a song they might like to share or a favourite quote or passage from a book.

Ask guests to each bring flowers for the altar and for everyone to wear something special – this is a nice way to mark the occasion.

YOU WILL NEED:

- *15 cardamom pods*
- *20 cloves*
- *3 teaspoons rosewater*
- *4 teaspoons agave nectar*
- *1 litre (34 fl oz/4 cups) water*

01 On the day, the host should prepare the tea at least an hour before the guests arrive so that everything is ready. Add all of the ingredients to a saucepan with full intention. As you drop each cardamom pod and clove in to the water, tell it a blessing that you wish you bring to your friends. Love, protection, happiness, joy, as you stir the tea in a clockwise direction bless it with kind words of intent. Bring to the boil and then simmer gently. Have a space set up with candles and incense burning.

02 As guests arrive, have everyone place their flowers on the altar – this should be a central space that you are all gathered around. Place the tea in a bowl in the middle of the altar – it should be coming straight off the stove, so it's nice and hot.

03 As everyone sits in a circle start with a mini guided meditation. The host or one of the guests could guide this through, or it is also totally fine to use a pre-recorded guidance.

04 The host should take the bowl of tea and take the first sip, then pass the bowl to the person next to them in a clockwise direction. As each person passes the bowl on they should offer their friend a blessing. Wish them well, an abundance of joy in their life, tell them why they love them and intentions that they wish for them.

05 If you wish, go around with the bowl and keep wishing each other blessings of love. Know that as you do this you are filling the tea with all of these good vibes and supportive, positive, heart-opening energy.

06 Now take time to go around the circle and share your stories, thoughts or creative projects. (Napkins for wiping the rim of the bowl are optional.)

SUNRISE AND SUNSET SPELLS

SUNRISE

Sunrise – the magical beginning of a brand new day. There is something very powerful and goose-bumpy about waking up early to cast a spell while everyone else is still asleep. Everything is so peaceful and the air is so fresh. Being up by yourself at this time can make you feel like you have the whole world to yourself. Just you, the sun and your magic!

As the sun rises, not only does it bring with it a brand new day, it brings powerful light that can be harnessed to assist with bringing fresh starts, abundance and to manifest major transformations.

Sun energy is great to work with if you're feeling a little stuck and need to call in on some enthusiasm in your life. You may be feeling like you are lacking inspiration, or maybe you are feeling a little lost and need a bit of sunlight to guide you in the right direction.

Call in on the sun's power to help cultivate ideas. What would you like to welcome in? Do you need to change your mindset? What are your dreams and visions of your future?

Use this sun energy to plant these seeds of intention, or if you are feeling a little foggy about what way your life is heading, use it to guide you and illuminate new opportunities to welcome into your life.

INSPIRATION AND ABUNDANCE SUN ENERGY ACTIVATOR SPELL

This spell is preferably done outdoors, facing east.

YOU WILL NEED:

- *a pinch of calendula or marigold leaves*
- *a pinch of frankincense resin*
- *a pinch of orris root powder*
- *a pinch of nutmeg*
- *a mortar and pestle*
- *a yellow candle*
- *a pen and paper*
- *a yellow pouch/cloth or yellow paper/ envelope*

---

01 Blend all of the herbs and resin, using a mortar and pestle, in a clockwise direction. Create this herbal blend with the intention of all of the abundance and inspiration you wish it to bring, the night before so that the herbs all get to know each other and can prepare themselves for their magical journey.

02 In the morning, just before the sun is rising, gather everything you will need for this spell. Be sitting peacefully, enjoy the silence for a moment and focus on what it is that you want this spell to bring you.

03 Burn the herbal blend following the hot charcoal guide on page 20. As the smoke travels, bathe the yellow candle in the smoke as the sun is rising and then light the candle.

04 As the candle burns, take your pen and paper and write what it is that you want to call in. Write it out as if you already have it. As you write, keep adding small pinches of your herbal blend to the charcoal. Know that these herbs are all being used to bring revelations and insights to help boost your confidence and guide you to a path of abundance. Trust what the smoke and sun energy is communicating with you at this time.

05 When you have finished writing, hold the paper over the magical smoke, thank the sun out loud for guiding you and shining light on your path. Fold the paper towards you three times in a clockwise direction.

06 Wrap the paper in a yellow cloth/pouch or yellow paper/envelope and keep it with you as a reminder of all the amazingness that is on its way to you.

SUNSET

As the sun is setting and day turns to night it is time to slow down, relax and honour your day.

Much like the energy of a waning moon, this is a time to tune inwards and connect with what is going on inside. Take time to unravel your thoughts of the day with an honest assessment – it is a time to celebrate the good and make peace with the bad.

Research shows that we have at least 50,000 thoughts a day. Obviously you can't recount every single one, but you can recognise which ones are working for you and helping you grow and which ones are holding you back from being your best self.

Getting in touch with our deeper selves can work as an amazing reset to help us enjoy our evening, make peace with our day and feel inspired about when the sun rises tomorrow.

This is a spell to help you tune in and give you courage to connect with your inner wisdom. Allow it to bless the best parts of your day and guide you through challenges you may have faced.

SUNSET REFLECTION
AND RELEASE RITUAL

Remember, all thoughts, both positive and negative, are welcome here!

YOU WILL NEED:

- *a pinch of sandalwood (or 5 drops of sandalwood essential oil)*
- *5 drops of jasmine essential oil*
- *5 cloves*
- *a pinch of copal resin*
- *a pen and paper*
- *a pestle and mortar*

---

01 Blend the sandalwood, jasmine, cloves and copal resin, using the mortar and pestle, in a clockwise direction. Burn the mix following the hot charcoal guide on page 20.

02 As you watch the smoke rise take some deep breaths. Know that the herbs are giving you the courage to connect to your truths and process your day.

03 When you feel ready, take your pen and paper and answer these questions. it is important not to overthink here; there is no right and no wrong – just write the first thing that pops into your mind.

- How am I feeling right now?
- What am I thankful for today?
- What inspired me today?
- What made me smile today?
- What did I daydream about today?
- What do I wish hadn't happened today?
- How do I feel stuck today?
- What do I need to surrender to right now?
- What stressed me out today and is this stressful situation beyond my control?
- How can I forgive myself today?
- Did I make someone smile today?
- How can I make someone smile tomorrow?
- How did I talk to myself today?
- How can I be kinder to myself?
- What signs and synchronicities did the Universe send me today?
- What are the kind words that I can say to myself right now?

04 There are two ways to expel the remnants of this spell. You may wish to burn this paper afterwards and release the day's energy. If you wish to do this, fold it three times away from you in an anti-clockwise direction. Or you may wish to keep it as a log and check in over a period of time.

SEASONAL WITCHCRAFT

We are nature, and as the seasons around us change so do we. When we tune in and work with seasonal energy we can often notice that what is going on in the outer world can be a true reflection of what is going on within us.

As these transformations happen in nature it is a good time to reflect and to connect with Mother Earth – solstices and equinoxes work as a guide for our personal growth. During these transitions we can allow the symbols of nature to remind us which areas in our lives might need exploring.

It is important to record how you feel as the seasons change – to notice what questions and feelings come up. Having a sense of personal awareness and honouring how we feel during these changeovers can remind us how connected to the Universe we are.

WINTER SOLSTICE

Winter solstice is officially the first day of winter and also marks the longest night of the year. This is also the time of year when the sun makes its official comeback; we may not be feeling its warmth for a few more months but we will be noticing its light (one minute extra per day to be precise!).

This is usually a time of deep reflection – think about what you will be leaving behind, what you will be bringing with you and what you wish to be calling in.

AS THE SUN IS REBORN SO ARE YOU!

WINTER SOLSTICE RITUAL

YOU WILL NEED:

- *a handful of fresh sage*
- *a handful of dried chamomile*
- *a pot of water*
- *candles*

Take a cleansing ritual bath the night before winter solstice.

Boil the herbs in a pot of water. As you do this and stir the pot, programme the herbs and tell them that you are calling in their power of renewal and change, and that you welcome them to wash away and cleanse you of what is no longer serving you for the coming new year. Leave the herbs to simmer for 20–30 minutes. If possible, leave the windows open as, while this is simmering on your stove, the scent is cleansing your house. When the herbs have infused in the water, allow it to cool down and then pour the water into a jug. (You can remove the herbs or leave them in the jug.)

Light some candles and run a bath or get the shower going. Know what it is that you are saying goodbye to, and, as you do this, pour your magical body wash over yourself. Know that you are cleansing yourself and are now ready to be reborn with the sun in the morning.

WINTER SOLSTICE SUNRISE SPELL

YOU WILL NEED:

- *a yellow or orange candle*
- *2 pinches of rosemary*
- *3 cloves*
- *a pinch of cinnamon*
- *a mortar and pestle*
- *a pen and paper*

Wake up for sunrise, face east as the sun is rising, and ring a bell, a sound bowl or shake a box of matches – let the Universe know that you are celebrating this coming back, welcoming warmth and light and growth into your life.

Light your orange candle to welcome back the sun, and blend the herbs, using a mortar and pestle following a clockwise direction. Once it's blended, follow the hot charcoal instructions on page 20 to get the smoke going. As the smoke travels, to honour the sun and bless your next cycle, take time to write out your intentions and celebrate what you will be carrying over from the past year.

- What has made you happy?
- What has brought you excitement and inspiration?
- What relationships bring you pure joy?
- What are your dreams for the year ahead?

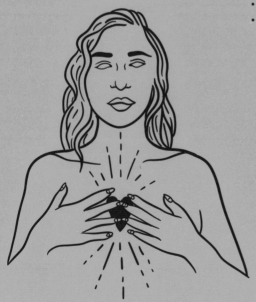

SPRING EQUINOX

Spring always seems to sneak up and, just when you feel like you can't handle another long winter's night or deal with another day of cold weather and layers of thermals (or is that just me?!), blossom starts to appear on trees, the days start getting longer and everyone has a spring in their step.

This is the time of year when Mother Earth reminds us that change is possible. A beautiful and bright reminder that as the seasons are constantly flowing and nature is making transitions from dark to light, we can too.

Embrace this energy and spring clean your home with the intention that you are clearing away the old to welcome in the new. Shake up any stagnant energy that has made itself at home during the long dark winter months – it is time to open your windows and let the sunlight in.

Begin with having a declutter and clearing out stuff you no longer need. Remember, everything holds energy and if you want to invite new energetic vibrations into your home you need to make room for them. If you have difficulty letting go of items, ask yourself if you would pay someone to look after it for six months. If you would then you should definitely keep it and if not... you know what to do!

Once you have decluttered make this magical cleansing detergent spell.

SPRING EQUINOX SPELL

YOU WILL NEED:

- *9 drops of sage essential oil*
- *9 drops of lavender essential oil*
- *1 tablespoon of an unscented carrier oil*
- *1 litre (34 fl oz/4 cups) hot water*

Mix the ingredients together and use it to wash all your surfaces.

After the downtime and hibernation of winter you may be raring to go, soaking up the fertile energy of the earth. This is a time to plant the seeds of your manifestations and get ready to watch them grow and blossom just like the trees. This is a great time to experiment, explore creative ideas, start projects and get yourself out there! This is a good time to plant seeds for yourself and for your garden. See page 34 for growing from seed.

SPRING EQUINOX RITUAL

YOU WILL NEED:
• *orange or yellow string or ribbon*
• *flowers and leaves*
• *crystals*
• *fruit*
• *a pen and paper*

Find your favourite tree, preferably one that is blossoming, and, using flowers, leaves, crystals, fruit or any other offering you may choose, create an altar beside the tree.

Write out your intentions and dreams of adventures you wish to welcome into your life and bury them in the centre of your altar. Leave the flowers and offerings at the tree (if you wish, you can bury your crystal with the paper). Before you leave, tie your string around one of the tree's branches three times. Every time you pass the tree and see your string, know that your wishes are on their way.

SUMMER SOLSTICE

This is the longest day of the year and is when the sun is at its strongest. When the sunbeams are so powerful, it's the perfect time to bless everything that's touched by its magical rays – from homegrown dried herb bundles and resins to talismans and crystals. It's also a very good moment to harvest your magical plants.

This is a time to recognise and give thanks for all the abundance in your life; call this fire energy in to be daring and take risks. Solar energy can help to push you out of your comfort zone, getting yourself out there in the world. If you are feeling a little lost, you can call in the sunshine to light the path that you should be on.

SUMMER SOLSTICE RITUAL

The sun rises around 4.30 a.m. (but check on the internet or weather forecast app for sunrise times where you live). Set your alarm clock super-early or, even better, stay up all night to welcome the sun in. This is the day that the sun's rays are at their most powerful, so you want to utilise this energy. Have all of your herbs, crystals and talismans, or anything else that you wish to bless (see page 22), set out along with a bell or a gong to ring at the moment the sun rises (maybe warn neighbours the night before!).

SUMMER SOLSTICE SUNRISE SPELL

YOU WILL NEED:

- *3 yellow candles*
- *a pinch of patchouli*
- *a pinch of dried marigold leaves*
- *a pinch of dried rose petals*
- *a pinch of cinnamon*
- *5 cloves*
- *a pen and paper*
- *a mortar and pestle*

Once the sun has begun to rise, light the yellow candles and blend the ingredients with a mortar and pestle, in a clockwise direction. You can do this in a larger quantity if you wish – a tablespoon of each, and 15 cloves – and leave out until noon to soak up all the rays. This is a great spell to have in the stockpile for the coming dark, winter months when you need some sun energy to brighten your days. Once it's blended, follow the hot charcoal guide on page 20 to get the smoke going, and then write down all the things that you are grateful for in your life; all of your abundances, your personal successes, your loves and what inspires you. This will act as a cosmic record of achievement, reminding you of all your spiritual successes to get you through the winter.

AUTUMN EQUINOX

This is when summer moves to autumn, and at this moment we have equal lengths of day and night. It's all about finding balance and harmony in your life. As it starts to get darker outside, we begin to look within ourselves, as well as connecting with nature. As the trees lose their leaves, we can use this moment to release what no longer serves us. This is also a reminder that every ending is followed by a new beginning. Coming out of the high energy of summer, this is a good time to take it easy, to rest and relax. It's important to restore ourselves before the incoming winter months; treat yourself to a massage, gather with friends to do face masks or exchange your favourite books.

AUTUMN EQUINOX RITUAL

As nature sheds a skin and moves to her next phase, so do we. A really nice way to release is to gather with friends around a firepit (or, if that's out of reach, a black candle). Set up the firepit or candle according to the space you have available and then each person should begin to write a goodbye letter to anything that is holding them back; be it a negative thought pattern, anxieties, money problems, or even toxic relationships or social media addiction. Fold the paper away from you three times, turning in an anti-clockwise direction with each fold. Throw your letter on the fire and know that what you have written is being released. It's time to say goodbye.

AUTUMN EQUINOX SPELL

If people have joined you around the firepit, it's nice to share a positive – I use the opportunity to **celebrate the foods of the season**, be it with hazelnut cookies or a root vegetable stew. Feel free to use your favourite recipe – the importance is to cook with intention. Stir your ingredients in a clockwise direction, to welcome in the grounding energy that this cycle will bring. This is one of my best friend's recipes; it sets an intention to share food with friends and to celebrate love and abundance within your relationships.

INGREDIENTS:

- *1 tablespoon ground chia seeds*
- *75 g (2½ oz) hazelnuts*
- *160 g (5½ oz/1½ cups) '00' flour*
- *100 g (3½ oz/ 1 cup) caster (superfine) sugar*
- *2 tablespoons olive oil*
- *pinch of lemon zest*
- *1 teaspoon baking powder*

Ryan and Francesca's Tozzetti

Preheat the oven to 180°C (350°F/Gas 6). Mix 4 tablespoons of water with the ground chia seeds and set aside to soak for 10 minutes. Whizz half the nuts into the flour and roughly cut the other half into large chunks. Mix the soaked chia seeds with the sugar then add the oil, hazelnut flour, lemon zest and baking powder. Mix to form a dough then turn out on to the countertop and form into two wide sausage shapes. Place in the oven and bake for 25–30 minutes. Remove, cool slightly, then slice diagonally into cookies. Return to the oven for 5 more minutes, then turn off the oven and leave the cookies inside until the oven has fully cooled down. This residual heat dries the cookies out so they can be stored for a long time in jars – to fully dry them out at a hotter temperature makes them go hard and not be crumbly.

WITCHCRAFT 101

This is a list of FAQs that commonly come my way. Read this section if you have a couple of queries, or if your magical mojo needs a little bit of a boost.

01 **I feel drawn to a spell, but it's the wrong moon phase, e.g. I want to banish something, but it's the time to call things in.**
Magic takes a little imagination. If you want to banish something, you don't have to wait for a waning moon – you can just call in the opposite of what you were going to banish. For example, if you have money worries, instead of dispelling your problem, call good fortune and abundance in.

02 **I want to do a seven-day candle spell, but I'm not sure when to blow it out.**
This is a very common question – in essence, the candle should be lit when you are present in the moment. Set up the candle, light it and blow it out after a couple of hours. Each night, revisit the spell and relight the candle. There's no need to continually burn the candle.

03 **I want to do a spell that will draw a particular person to me, or have an effect on someone else.**
This is where the ethics of magic come into play. You have to ask yourself how you would feel if someone was doing a spell to influence your energy. Therefore, I always say it's best to keep your focus on your own emotions and actions.

04 **I really want to do a spell, but I don't like the herbs in the mix.**
It's important that you feel a positive connection with your ingredients. If you have an allergy or a negative association with a herb or essential oil, then don't use it – refer to the glossary for alternatives, pages 42–43.

05 **I can't grow magical herbs, is it ok to use dried ones straight from the kitchen cupboard?**
It's always best to use herbs that you have blessed and programmed, and specifically stored for your spell work (page 41). But if you are a witch on the go, gather the herbs from your kitchen and say out loud to them what they are being used for. Even better, give them a quick bathe in frankincense essential oil.

06 **I can't find a particular crystal, is it OK to use alternatives?**
In short, yes – a clear quartz is multi-purpose. Just remember to tell the crystal about the specific job you want it to do – they are great little listeners.

07 **I love practising magic, but none of my friends are into it.**
It can sometimes be a little lonely when exploring magic – but there are still ways you can swap magical stories and continue on your journey. My top tip would be to find a spiritual shop or centre near you, and go along to a workshop or event. If you are feeling nervous, take a crystal of courage in your pocket. Social media is a great way of

connecting, too. And remember, your vibe attracts your tribe.

08 I'm finding it hard to trust my intuition.
Remember that you need to be feeling calm and grounded to receive a clear answer. Give yourself time and patience. For a quick fix, rub rosemary on your third eye.

09 Why isn't my spell working?
Magic works in mysterious ways. The Universe is always looking out for you to provide you with the best possible outcomes. If your magic isn't working, it could be because you are being protected. It could mean that you are not ready, or it could be that something bigger and better is on the way. This is the reason why it is always a good idea to keep a record of your spells and the dates the magic was performed.

10 I want to practice magic, but I feel like I never have time.
The thing with magic is, it is important to create time. Saying that, it is also really easy to add a bit of magic into your daily life – a body scrub in the shower or a few positive intentions when cooking will make all the difference.

11 How do I better protect myself from negative energies?
Close your eyes and think of a colour that makes you feel safe and protected – there are no rights or wrongs here. Imagine the light surrounding your body and shining bright, feeling it wrap around you like a secure cuddle. Know that when you are surrounded by this light, no harm can come to you.

12 I did a playing card tarot reading but I didn't like the answer.
This is the time to ask yourself why you didn't like the answer. Was it posing a question that made you look at things in a different way? Is there another way that this card can be interpreted? Take some time and revisit the reading in a few days to see if it resonates then. Remember that there is always a reason, even if it isn't immediately clear.

13 My friend is sad and I want to do a spell for them.
If you want to create a positive spell to help somebody, it is a lovely thing, but you should always ask for permission before you do it. You can also take a lock of their hair to connect them to it, and if you are performing it at home without them being present, visualise them or place a photo of them at your altar.

14 I want to make a spell, but I don't have any privacy.
In this situation, imagination is needed. Perhaps you could go to the park, or take a look at the spell and see how you can simplify it. Ultimately, you can do most things with a pen and paper, if needs must. And remember that the moon is capable of supercharging and blessing your written-down manifestations, so timing can help, too. Read about sigils on pages 114–115, and an altar on the go on page 23.

15 I really love magic, but I'm scared of doing it wrong.

The number one thing to remember is that if your intentions are good and the magic that you are wishing to create is coming from a positive place, then there's no such thing as making a mistake.

16 I've lost my faith, how do I get it back?

It might not feel like it at the time, but losing your faith is always an opportunity to find it again on a deeper level. Usually, this means that there is some healing to be done. Just be gentle and kind to yourself, and know that it will return in good time. See page 114 for a surrender sigil.

17 What if I don't have a bath?

If you are wanting to use essential oils, add them to a piping hot wash cloth and leave in the corner of the shower – the steam will infuse the aroma. Or if they are herbs and flowers, wrap them in a muslin and tye the ends together and hang the muslin below the shower head so that the water can run through it.

18 What should I say to people who don't believe in magic?

To anybody who questions magic, I usually say, that the power of human connections, and the ways in which we engage with nature around us is to me, the clearest demonstration of the existence of magic that I can think of. This is pure magic, in every way.

INDEX

A

abundance
crystals for 99
welcoming abundance vaporiser mix 127
air 24, 50, 149
altars 22–4
animal omens 192
Aquarius 92–3
Aries 86
astrological moon rituals 85–93
autumn equinox 214–15

B

bath oils 123
bathing ritual 89
bird omens 190, 192
blending 17
blessing 17
body oils 124
body scrubs 120

C

Cancer 88
candles 46–53
burning 52
colour 51
dressing 51–2
extinguishing 53
pyromancy 52–3
seven-day candle spell 216
spells 51–3, 216
Capricorn 92
cartomancy 158–9
ceremonies 194–205
chakras 54–67

challenges
daily challenges 128–39
daily gratitude challenge 139
seven-day ritual challenge 132–7
charcoal, hot 20
chariology 144–57
clarity, crystals for 102
cleansing
herbs 41
smoke cleansing 44–5
clothes, empowering 16
club cards 168
colour, candles 51
connection spell 87
cookies, Ryan and Francesca's tozzetti 215
cosmic cuddle body oil 124
crown chakra 57, 66
crystals 94–103, 216
for abundance & prosperity 99
classical elements and 24
crystal activation 98–103
for focus and clarity 102
for healing and grounding 101
herbs, woods and resins pairings 33
for love and relationships 103
for protection 100
storing 97

D

daily challenges 128–39
diamond cards 165
divination 140–93

E

ears 192
earth 24, 50, 149
elements, classical 24
empowerment, outfit of 16

enchanting 17
herbs 40–1
enlivening and rejuvenation bath oil 123
equinoxes
autumn equinox 214–15
spring equinox 210–11
eyes, omens and 192

F

faith, losing 218
fate line 152
feet 192
fingers, reading 147, 152
fire 24, 50, 148
flame reading 52–3
flexibility, hands 147
focus, crystals for 102
fortune telling 140–93
Friday ritual challenge 136–7
friendship circle group tea ceremony 200–1

G

Gemini 87
'get up and go' spell 92
goals, writing down 108–11
gratitude challenge, daily 139
grounding
crystals for 101
grounding spell 87

H

hands
omens 192
palmistry 144–57
head line 151
headspace 16
healing
crystals for 101
healing energy vaporiser mix 127

ABOUT
THE AUTHOR

Semra Haksever was a fashion stylist for over a decade before starting Mama Moon, a bespoke collection of magical scented candles and potions. Semra hosts spell-making workshops and moon-manifesting ceremonies teaching people how to empower themselves and feel good with the help of a little magic.

She has practised reiki, crystal therapy and moon rituals for over 20 years, and has always held the desire to create ritualistic tools that are accessible to all. This is her third book.

MAMAMOONCANDLES.COM

ABOUT THE
ILLUSTRATOR

Nes Vuckovic is a Bosnian-born, Chicago-based illustrator and visual artist focussed primarily on clean linework, surreal juxtaposition and the female form.

A self-appointed pastel queen, her work often reverts back to her blackwork roots, having primarily focused on cartooning and graphic novels in her formal arts education.

She's a B-Horror movie, taxidermy and sci-fi enthusiast. Pitbull lover. Overly dramatic. Lifetime movie, wine and cheese fanatic.

ACKNOWLEDGEMENTS

Simon, my darling dream man, I dedicate this book to you. Thank you for embracing magic and always supporting and encouraging my witchy ways. You are my living proof that magic works. I love you with all my heart and you are no1 on my gratitude lists forever!

Sei la mia vita!!!

Heres to you, me, Cher and the cockroaches XXX

I am aware that these acknowledgements get a little acceptance speechy, but without the love of all these amazing kind-hearted, magical friends and family I wouldn't be who I am and this book would never have been written, so my love and gratitude goes out to (in no particular order!!!) to my Mummy, Tarik, Suwindi, Ma, Ayalah, Banos, Jackson, Debs, Dominique, Trisha, Sam and The OMOS... and of course, the amazing team at Hardie Grant for embracing magic. Kate, thank you so much for everything, you rock! Eve, I literally couldn't have done this without you and I am so full of gratitude for all your help (and the croissants!!) and Nes and Claire for making it look so cosmic and cool. X

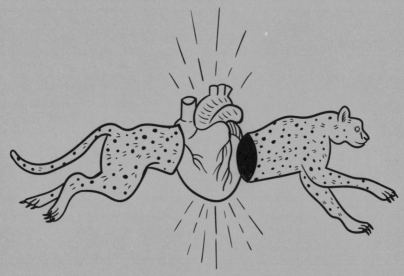

Published in 2020 by Hardie Grant Books,
an imprint of Hardie Grant Publishing

Hardie Grant Books (London)
5th & 6th Floors
52–54 Southwark Street
London SE1 1UN

Hardie Grant Books (Melbourne)
Building 1, 658 Church Street
Richmond, Victoria 3121

hardiegrantbooks.com

British Library Cataloguing-in-
Publication Data. A catalogue record
for this book is available from the
British Library.

Mama Moon's Book of Magic
by Semra Haksever

ISBN: 978-1-78488-274-7
10 9 8 7 6 5

Publishing Director: Kate Pollard
Senior Editor: Eve Marleau
Design: Claire Warner Studio
Illustrations: Nes Vuckovic
Editor: Lisa Pendreigh
Proofreader: Gregor Shepherd
Indexer: Vanessa Bird

Colour Reproduction by p2d
Printed and bound in China by
Leo Paper Products Ltd.